Happy Trails
To You!
Ollie Hill

Packing and Outfitting Field Manual

Fifth Edition

by Oliver (Ollie) C. Hill

ISBN: 0-9763342-0-8

Library of Congress Cataloging-in-Publication 2004195171

Cover photo by Wyoming Travel and Tourism—the Wagner Perspective

Printed by Pioneer Printing and Stationery Co. Inc., Cheyenne, Wyoming

Cover design by Elizabeth Ono-Rahel, Laramie, Wyoming

4-76/5M/.40 1-80/2M/.85 8-81/4M/.61 3-89/10M/1.45 12-04/6M/1.87

Dedicated to my friend **Jim Talbott**

Jim was a rancher and outdoorsman extraordinaire. He was the founder of Savage Run Outfitters and co-teacher of our horse packing schools. He was very proud of the quality cattle, mules and horses he raised. He had a tremendous will to live and to make life better for others, especially for his children, grandchildren and friends. Jim was a great family man to his wife, Janet; five grown children, Jay, Amy, Scott, Cody and Betsy; and six grandchildren, all of whom he truly adored. He passed away on October 21, 2004, after suffering three years with cancer. On that day this book went to the printer. He will be missed by all who knew him.

CONTENTS

PREFACE

The purpose of this *Packing and Outfitting Field Manual* is to provide basic information in an organized manner to help you learn about pack animals, packing equipment, as well as how to effectively plan and take pack trips in the great outdoors. Use of qualified persons to help with the teaching of packing fundamentals, and references such as this manual, will make packing easier and more fun.

Major objectives of this manual are as follows:

1. To show and explain the types of camping and horse equipment needed for packing.

2. To demonstrate how to tie packing hitches properly - half diamond, single diamond, double diamond, squaw hitch, basket sling, barrel sling and Arizona hitch. Also how to tie on a sheepherder stove, bucket, pack meat and tie off a hitch.

3. To illustrate and assist you in learning how to tie properly the 21 knots shown in this manual.

4. To show food and equipment lists applicable to groups of different sizes.

5. To outline principles of setting up trip itineraries.

6. To emphasize human and horse first aid kits for on-the-trail care.

7. To stress the importance of knowing the basics of wilderness survival.

8. To create an awareness about Wyoming Game and Fish, USDA Forest Service, Bureau of Land Management and the Wyoming State Board of Outfitters and Professional Guides regulations and licenses governing packing and outfitting as a business.

9. To show a variety of photos and drawings to assist in understanding and learning about packing and outfitting.

For orders and information on professional packing schools, call or write:

Oliver (Ollie) C. Hill
330 Pahlow Lane
Laramie, Wyoming 82070
Phone: 307-745-4553
E-mail: ollie_wy@hotmail.com

Trade or brand names are used only for the purpose of educational information. The information given herein is supplied with the understanding that no discrimination is intended and no endorsement is implied.

See order form for High Country Horse, LLC items, page 117.

ACKNOWLEDGMENTS

Appreciation is expressed to those who helped plan, conduct and work with the original packing and outfitting course and manual in 1970 and to those who contributed information and photographs in this and earlier manuals.

• Al Richardson, Colorado State University, riding and packing instructor, who taught and inspired the writer to create the original manual in 1970 and the four revisions leading to this fifth edition.

• Many friends in the San Luis Valley who helped with the packing courses and with the field manual: Bob and Judy Irvine, Roy Pattison and his staff, 4-H Leaders and San Luis Valley Outfitters.

• Wyoming Game and Fish, USDA Forest Service, Wyoming State Board of Outfitters and Professional Guides and Bureau of Land Management for information and regulations.

• Heather Smith Thomas, for information on "Staking Out" taken from *Appaloosa News*, January 1970, p. 70, by special permission.

• University of Wyoming staff and faculty - Ruth Moe, Dana Drienhofer, Nancy Nichols, Herb Pownall, Randy Anderson, Dr. E. Lee Belden, Delores Bixby, Bob Trumbull and Graphic Arts Service.

• My wife Joyce for computer and photography help, and son Lynn and daughter Crystal for their understanding and support.

• D.P. Nicholson, D.V.M., for abundant horse first aid information and Melanie Manning, D.V.M., and Clay Lilley, D.V.M., for revisions to horse first aid information.

• Jim Talbott and son Jay Talbott owners of Savage Run Outfitters.

• Dave Mathis, Reno, Nevada, for some drawings.

• Back Country Horsemen, Columbia Falls, Montana, for photo.

• Colin and Ruth Kaltenbach for the sourdough pancake recipe.

• Doug Reynolds, University of Wyoming extension agent, Rawlins, Wyoming, for packing photographs and information on restraints.

• Businesses that supplied information on packing equipment; The Boardwalk, Laramie, Wyoming; Ralide and Ralide West, West Yellowstone, Montana; Tall Oak Tree Outfitting Supply Inc., Cody, Wyoming; Brighton Feed and Tack, Brighton, Colorado; Custom Pack Rigging, Lillooet, British Columbia; and Rollin Beauchane Manufacturing Co., Canby, Oregon.

• Gary Keimig of Western Wilderness Studio, Dubois, Wyoming, for camp painting of DuNoir Wilderness Camp and drawing of bull elk.

INTRODUCTION

HISTORY OF PACKING

Packing as we know it and as history has shown, was developed in the neighborhood of 700 years ago when Mongolia's Genghis Khan used pack animals. Khan's nomads were extremely tough hands who traveled fast, using hit and run tactics. The speed with which the Mongolians traveled, their use of extra horses for relays and their transportation of captives and loot – all point to great skill and knowledge in packing.

Some 200 years after Genghis Khan, the Spaniards brought the first mules and horses to the New World. In their pillage tactics, they too, had to transport cargoes and supplies of different kinds. With the combination of the Spaniard's "horse know-how" and the invention of gunpowder, it is little wonder the American Indians had great difficulties with the people coming into the New World.

From Cortez's landing in 1519 to Jim Bridger's trapping expeditions in the Rocky Mountains and the era of the trappers, traders and pioneers of the West, horses and packing played an important part in the development of the United States.

According to Joe Back, author of *Horses, Hitches and Rocky Trails,* more of the methods and equipment came from the Spanish than from any other source. But the American Indians also used animals for packing, starting with dogs for backpacking and hauling a travois. When they discovered the wild, four-legged horse, they received a new lease on life and some undreamed-of possibilities as far as packing was concerned.

From all these evolvements and knowledge about the horse, modern day equipment, as we know it, has been developed. Pack saddles, rawhide covered trees and many other items were inherited from Spanish, English and French explorers.

Other packing history goes back many centuries to Europe, where pack trains were used to transport merchandise on the backs of mules, donkeys and horses. In England even in the 1700s, roads were not well developed, so people had to rely on animals for packing. As the far western United States opened up, packing became more important as pack animals were used by trappers, hunters and prospectors. In the Gold Rush days, ore, supplies and machinery were packed into the rugged western mountain country. That was when packing became a trade and profession in its own right.

Even now, in spite of modern transportation, there is still considerable packing done in remote areas. Most is done for recreation: hunting, fishing, camping and sightseeing trips.

SELECTION OF THE PACK ANIMAL

Selection of a pack animal is very important. Your pack animal is a critical part of any involvement with packing and outfitting. Many people believe the sure-footed **mule** is one of the more desireable animals for packing. He uses his food to good advantage and will not hurt himself. In many parts of the country, horses are used and burros frequentely are used for smaller packs. **Burros** cannot travel as rapidly as can a horse or mule. They have a calm disposition, but they can be stubborn. The burro works well if the packer plans to walk and lead him rather than lead from a saddle horse. The **llama** is becoming popular as a sure-footed partner on pack trips, especially where people walk and lead their pack animals. Dogs and goats are also seen on the trails with backpackers.

In the selection of a pack animal, one should keep in mind that he should be stout and rugged and have sound feet and legs. He should have a gentle disposition and should be healthy. Fairly prominent, but not overly prominent withers are desirable to keep a saddle and pack from slipping from side to side. Caution needs to be used with sawbuck pack saddles on high-withered animals, as the pack tends to ride down on the top of the withers and can pinch and cause saddle sores due to lack of clearance. Most pack animals stand nearly 14 hands high, but size varies. Shorter animals are somewhat easier to pack for shorter people.

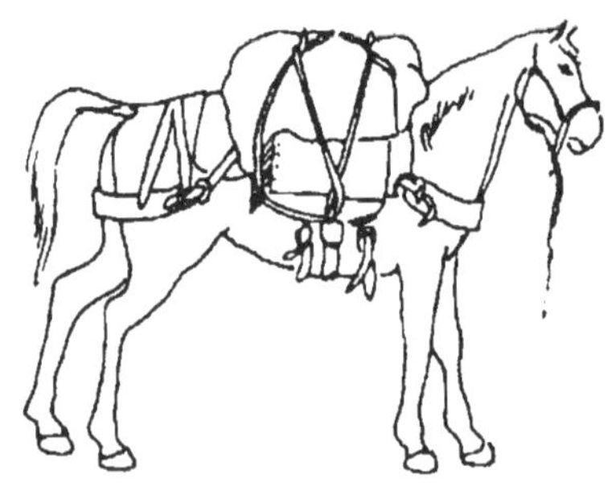

Key considerations are:

1. Gentle disposition.
2. Stout and rugged conformation.
3. Sound feet and legs.
4. Healthy - no coughs, sores or lameness.
5. Prominent withers, but not overly prominent.
6. An animal standing 14 hands or less for easy packing.
7. Mules and burros carry about 15 percent of their body weight while horses, about 12.5 percent.

CARE OF THE PACK ANIMAL

A pack animal, as well as a riding animal, should be well cared for and should be brushed, fed and not abused.

One should remember that the pack on a horse is actually dead weight; therefore, the pack is more difficult for the horse to carry and handle than to carry a rider, whose weight helps the horse as he moves. This necessitates extra care and checking of the animal's back and girth area for galls and irritations. Pad the animal well with a thick wool blanket and heavy pad. Both should be kept clean and soft and properly set without wrinkles. Cinches on pack animals should be kept tight to keep the pack from shifting, causing galls and back soreness. The use of sheepskin sleeves over the cinch will greatly reduce sores and galls. Many new materials for cinches and pads are available and need to be considered. Much care needs to be given to prevent your animal from developing sores. **Preventing sores is easier than healing them.** Care must be given to the feet by proper trimming and shoeing. Inspect the girth, back and elbow area every night and morning, testing for sore spots. If open sores develop, wash out with salt water before medicating. For hot spots and swollen areas, cold packs can be used to treat these areas.

BASIC PACKING EQUIPMENT

Good pack equipment is essential to an enjoyable trip and should include the following:

1. The pack saddle.
2. A heavy, clean saddle pad and wool blanket.
3. A stout halter with a lead rope at least 10' to 12' long.
4. The lash cinch, with a 45' lash rope (1/2" diameter).
5. The pack cover or manta (manti or manty) can vary in size from 6' x 6' up to 10' x 12', depending on multiple uses intended. The cover should be waterproof and quiet (polytarps are noisy).
6. A 20' to 30' coil of 1/4" or 3/8" rope works well to tie a manta over a bale, bedroll or tent.
7. Panniers, in good repair. Adjustable straps are helpful.
8. Stout, clean lash ropes and cinches (to be safe, carry a spare lash cinch).
9. Hobbles are essential for pack trips.

Types of panniers are highly variable. There is the rawhide pannier, wooden box or grub pannier and the popular canvas pannier of various types. The canvas type can be open, have a cover or be of the stock saddle type and be connected to drape over a riding saddle. Aluminum, ralide, cordura and other new materials and bear-proof panniers have all added new dimensions to packing. Duffle bags can be helpful for packing clothes and other personal gear. Hobbles for each animal and one bell for the "boss" animal are also essential equipment. If staking out is preferred over hobbles, the lash ropes can double as stake ropes. The stake rope, however, can get wet or freeze in a mountain meadow during the night or even break, so use caution.

There are many variations of equipment. In pack saddles, there is the common sawbuck or crossbuck saddle, the old army McClellan type, the Decker, the old Spanish style and the Indian pack saddle made from deer or elk horns. Stock saddles may also be used for packing. Each type of saddle can have several variations/models for certain purposes.

Proper adjustment of all equipment for the pack animal is necessary. The breeching straps need to be adjusted to prevent saddle and load from riding too far forward on the withers of the animal. The breast strap or collar is used to keep the weight of the pack and saddle from riding too far back on the horse's kidneys and back, which could cause back soreness. The breast collar should not be so tight as to cut off the horse's wind – or the breeching so tight that the animal cannot walk out properly. Be sure that the pack saddle cinch is tight before putting on the pack, or you may have to stop and re-do your pack at a difficult place on the trail.

LOADING AND PACKING

When preparing a load for an animal, you should weigh and balance the panniers to keep the pack from slipping or shifting and making the pack animal sore. The panniers should be loaded equally, and, to assure this balance of load, a small set of hand scales is helpful. The **heavy items** should be loaded on the bottom of the pack to help maintain a low center of gravity. **Breakable items** should be put in bags or metal or plastic containers to prevent breakage in the pack. Lighter items, such as bedrolls or feed, could be placed on top of the pack saddle and between the panniers, then covered by the manta to protect the entire pack. Equipment, such as an axe, saw, bucket or shovel can be packed on top of the manta and lashed onto the lash rope to be readily available. Some of these items can be carried in a rifle scabbard on your saddle horse.

A typical pile of gear to be arranged and loaded.

Stack your gear by the pack animal you will be using. Weigh each pannier, and make sure the load is balanced or there may be trouble on the mountain with an uneven pack. Considering the animal's **center of gravity** is important to avoid sores and to make carrying the load as comfortable and balanced as possible. Most animals' center of gravity will be 6" to 10" below their tail head from front to rear. Overly high packs or panniers loaded heavier in the bottom will cause an unbalance to the center of gravity. Just a reminder to consider these things when packing up.

BALANCING THE LOAD

Weight and balance of the panniers is very important to avoid sores on your pack animal. Panniers should be weighed and then the total load balanced carefully. Adjust the height of the load, front to rear and side to side on each pannier.

ON THE TRAIL

On a pack trip, the pack animal should receive priority treatment. He should be loaded last and when stopping to camp, he should be unloaded first.

If tailing the string together, it is important to know the animals that get along and those that don't. Tie accordingly and you will avoid some wrecks. There are numerous ways to tie a pack string together on the trail. A tail knot to tail up horses in a string may be used, with care. They may be tied by the lead rope to the D-ring of the pack saddle of the horse in front or tied to a pigtail loop from the pack saddle. Tie short enough so the lead rope does not get under the lead horse's tail or trouble may start. It is best to lead the pack stock rather than to turn them loose. **One precaution:** The rider on the lead horse should never tie a pack horse solid to his or her saddle horn. This is asking for trouble since the rider would be unable to get the lead rope loose in case of a wreck. Instead, the rope should be dallied around the saddle horn a turn or two with the packer holding the loose end in his or her hand (gloves are better than rope burns) for immediate release if needed. The rope can be held in the hand if the lead pack animal leads out easily and is well-broke to lead.

Caution: Ropes can be dangerous. Except when using a rope as a lariat, there should be no loops in it because of the danger of getting a foot or hand caught and being dragged. Care must be taken to avoid getting hands or feet caught in rope coils. You never know when a "rodeo" may start and you might get caught in the middle. Be cautious and alert, and play it safe with ropes.

TRAIL COURTESY

A smile and a friendly "hello" or "howdy" will go a long way in the back country to create an attitude of courtesy and cooperation.

Observe the basics:

- In steep rough country, downhill traffic usually yields to uphill traffic, but if you have a better place to pull off the trail, please do so and let others pass by.
- People with llamas, on foot or on mountain bikes should yield to pack animals, because it is easier for people to move off the trail. If they don't, smile and yield the trail. Then ask them to stand below the trail and wait quietly for your animals to pass.

Practice Makes Perfect

Use a miniature pack horse, a barrel or box for practicing hitches at home. See order form for Do It Yourself Plans, page 117.

PACKING AS A HOBBY

Packing as a hobby or as a business, can be enjoyable with the proper horse equipment, a basic knowledge of the horse, good camping equipment, a sound trip itinerary, well-thought-out menus and other details that together make a well-rounded pack trip.

Use this *Packing and Outfitting Field Manual* to help you become more proficient at tying hitches and knots; preparing equipment; developing food lists and menus; working with itineraries; developing horse and human first aid kits; gaining an appreciation for and knowledge about wilderness survival; and learning about the many aspects of packing.

This information has been prepared for 4-H leaders and members, guides and outfitters, hunting and fishing friends, Wyoming Game and Fish and USDA Forest Service and Bureau of Land Management personnel, as well as anyone interested in the outdoors and packing as a hobby or a business. It will be a useful reference on the trail, as well as at home. You are invited to insert your own comments, suggestions, ideas and "tricks of the trade" to help improve your packing and outfitting experiences. Each individual and situation is different, so the contents of this manual should be adapted and molded to fit your specific needs.

Best of luck, hunters, fishermen, sightseers, outfitters, guides and other adventurers. Learn, enjoy and avoid those potential wrecks on the trail.

THE HORSEMAN'S CREED

When I ride out of the mountains, I'll leave only hoof prints, take only memories.

CHAPTER 1

PACK TRIP EQUIPMENT AND SUPPLIES

Types of Horse Equipment
- Rigging Your Own Pack Saddles
- Pack Saddle Improvement Ideas

Essential Equipment - Axe, Shovel, Bucket and Saw
Lists and Weights
- Camping Equipment
  - Tents
  - Camping Gear
- Horse Feed
- Other Horse Equipment
- Cooking Equipment
- First Aid Supplies - Human
  - Horse
- Personal Gear
- Food - Menus
  - Recipes
  - Food List
- The Weight Factor
- Pack Horses Needed

Packing Up
Pack Animal Speed Index

TYPES OF HORSE EQUIPMENT

Saddles

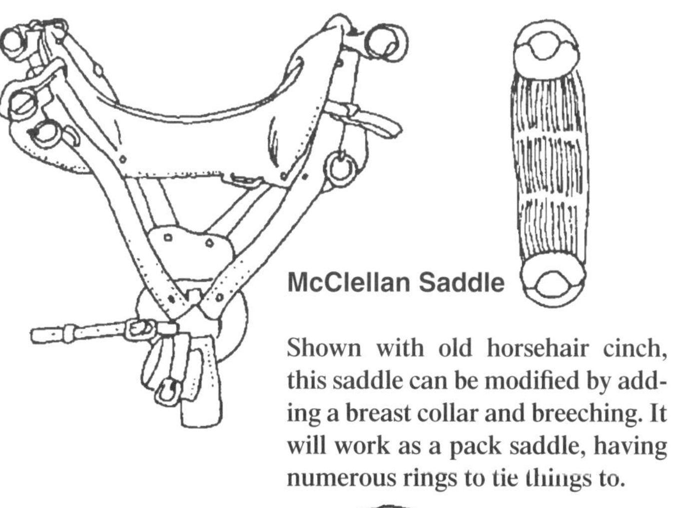

McClellan Saddle

Shown with old horsehair cinch, this saddle can be modified by adding a breast collar and breeching. It will work as a pack saddle, having numerous rings to tie things to.

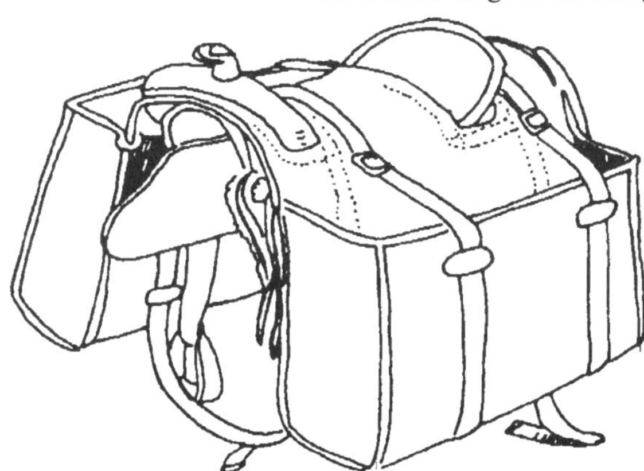

Stock Saddle Panniers

These can be rolled up and tied behind your saddle and carried until you are ready to use them. Most have straps over the top and under the belly.

Sawbuck or Crossbuck Saddle

Photo shows the extra length of a pack pad and the double pack cinch that is braided together. Both are good investments.

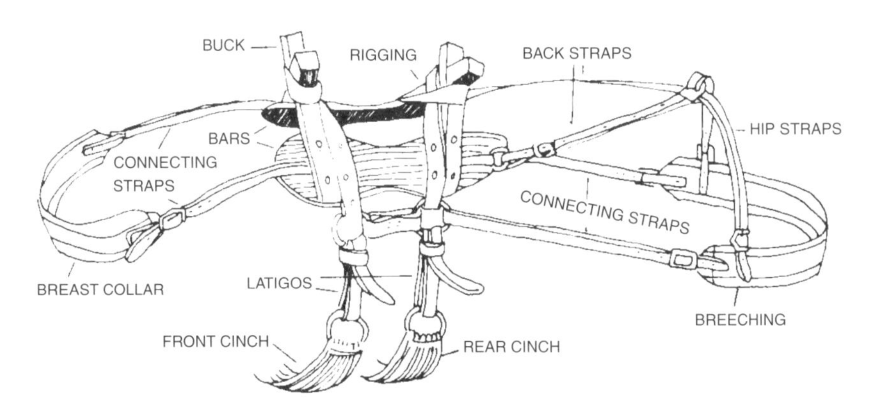

You can add sheepskin lining on the bars to give your pack animal a lot more protection.

Rigging Your Own Pack Saddles

If you are a "do it yourself" person, you may consider buying a basic tree and rigging it yourself. You might buy a basic crossbuck or a decker tree to start, or you may want to consider some of the new trees on the market. You may want to consider a fully adjustable crossbuck/sawbuck type tree with adjustable or fixed arches. The arches pivot on the bars and float to fit each animal's back and withers. Some trees are available with up to four styles of bars, where each is shaped to fit animals with different types of backs.

The big advantages of these trees is more of a custom fit to your pack animal, causing fewer sores. They can be adjusted to fit different animals also.

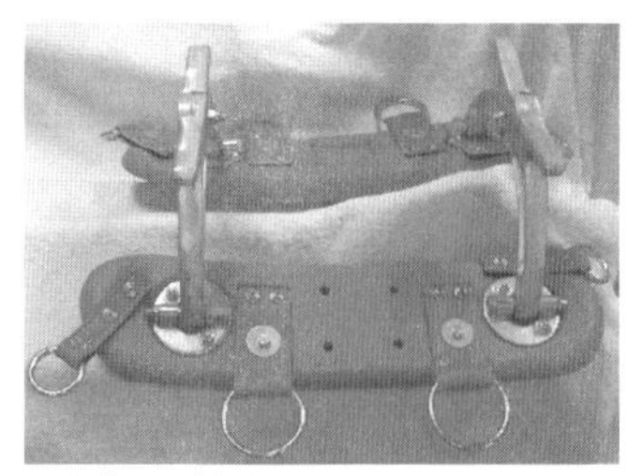

Adjustable Sawbuck Type Tree

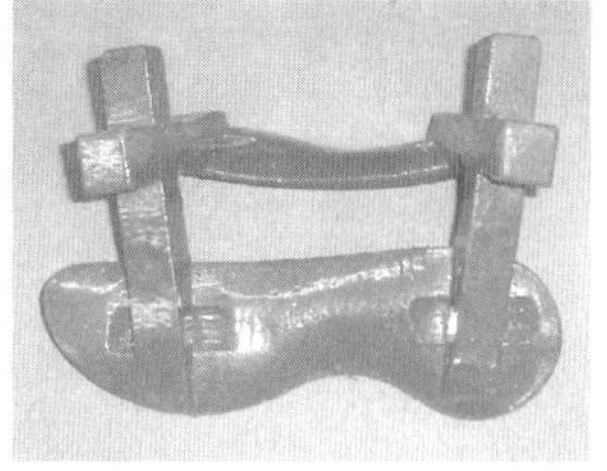

Coated Crossbuck Saddle Tree

Another consideration could be the basic crossbuck tree that has been coated with a tough material similar to that used in truck beds. Advantages are toughness, easier rigging, more weather proof and less maintenance.

Using a fully skirted pack saddle tree is another good option to consider if you rig your own saddle.

Contact your local tack shop for details on these and other innovations in the packing and outfitting industry.

Pack Saddle Improvement Ideas

Sheepskin lining (1), quarter straps (2) and a four-strap butt plate (3) are a few ways you may want to improve your saddles if they are not built with these items.

Regular sheepskin saddle lining can be glued and tacked on the bars of a crossbuck saddle to give additional padding for your pack animal.

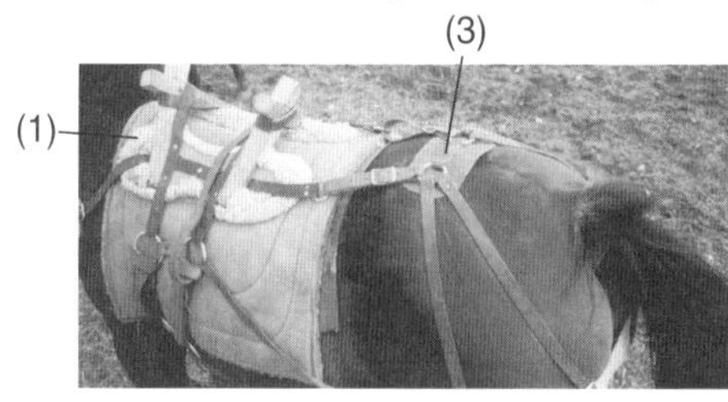

A butt plate provides strength to the breeching area, and it rides better on top of the animal's croup. The four hip straps provide more stability to the breeching, so it rides more evenly behind the horse.

Quarter straps are very helpful to pull the front cinch back from the animal's elbow area to help reduce sores. Note: The near side strap must always be unsnapped before unsaddling.

See order form for Do It Yourself Plans, page 117.

Double Rigged

The connected double cinch is great for packing. It helps keep the back cinch from sliding back and causing a rodeo.

Decker Saddle

Single Rigged and Adjustable

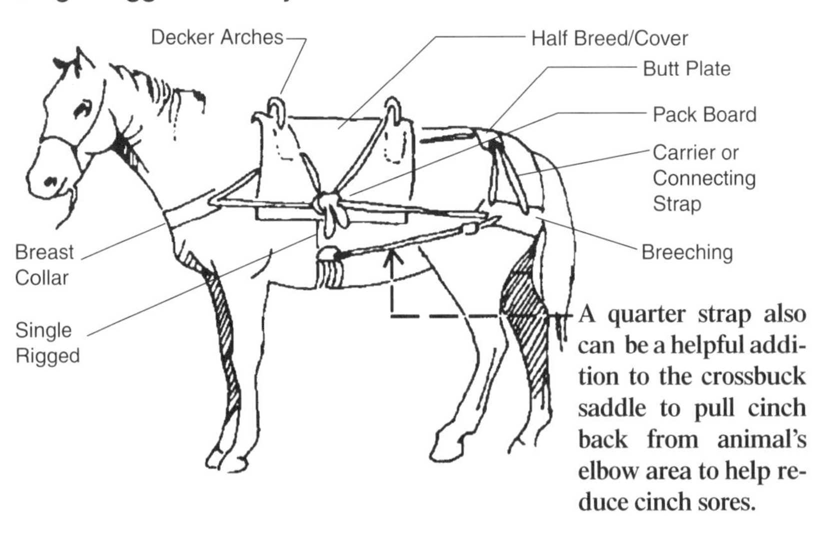

A quarter strap also can be a helpful addition to the crossbuck saddle to pull cinch back from animal's elbow area to help reduce cinch sores.

Note: Be sure to remove the balled up hair and mud from the saddle pad, blanket and cinch before saddling to prevent sores.

Panniers

Wooden Box or Grub Panniers

Box panniers can also be covered with fiberglass. It's best if they are beveled to fit the animals's side. Shelves and compartments are handy. They also can double as a small table in camp.

Rawhide Panniers

Stretch a fresh cowhide over the 1/2" steel rod framework beveled to fit horse's side. These panniers are rugged and also heavy. Sew with nylon cord. See order form for Do It Yourself Plans, page 117.

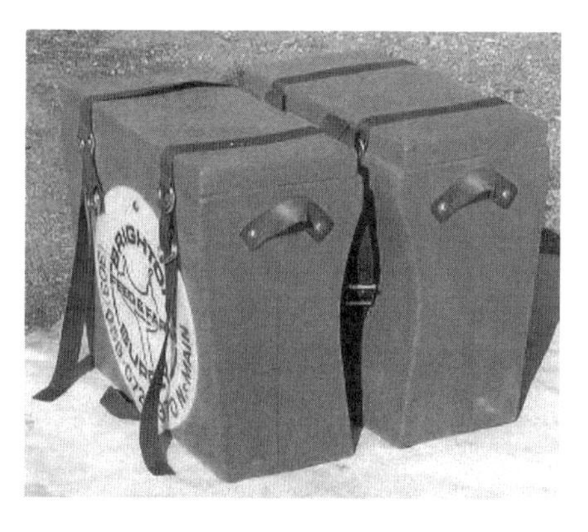

Poly/Fiberglass Panniers

New tough materials lend to a variety of well-made, durable panniers. Lids make these even more usable in camp and keep out the mice.

Army Surplus can be a great source for "do-it yourselfers." Army cargo bags can be sewn together to make a tough pannier.

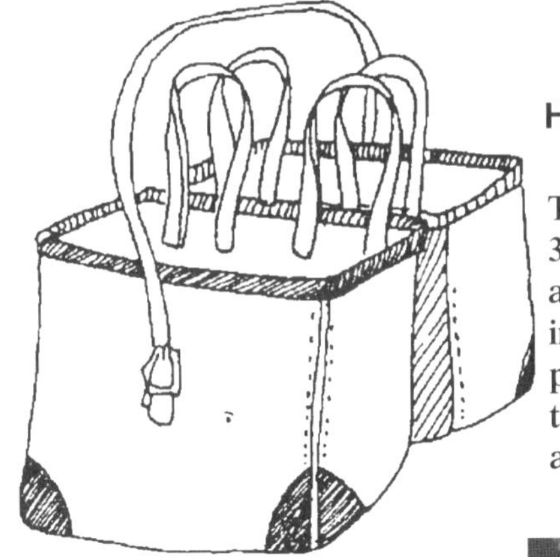

Heavy Canvas Pannier

These panniers are shown with 3/8" rope sewn into the top edge and a strap over top to hold sleeping bags, tents or other items packed on top. Buckles added to the hanger straps make them more adjustable.

Aluminum Kitchen Pannier

Various types of metal panniers are now available. This one doubles as a stove and others form a complete kitchen.

New bear-proof aluminum panniers are required in bear country.

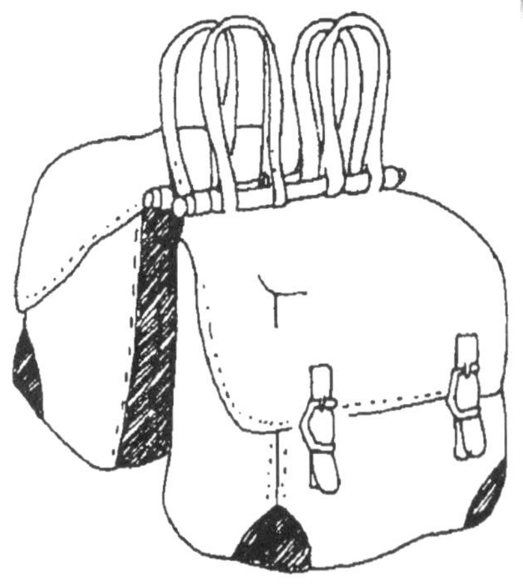

Canvas and Leather Pannier

This type is made with pipe or dowel and a lid. There also are all leather panniers of this type. Some have leather ends, others have leather corners. New lightweight materials like cordura are excellent as well.

Straps, rings and buckles all enhance these basic panniers. Buckles in the pannier loops help adjust the load. Straps over the top hold the top pack, and straps and smaller cinches underneath help secure the load. Rings are always useful to tie to, so add them wherever appropriate.

Pad

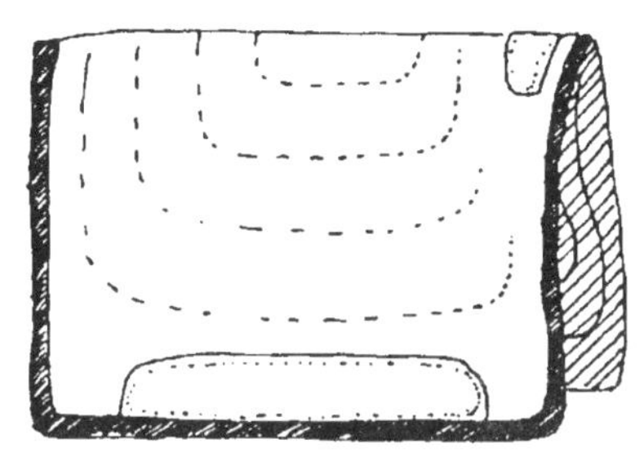

Use an extra long pad for the pack animals, up to 30" x 48" compared to a standard pad of 30" x 30". This gives protection to the animal's side if panniers or lash rope happen to rub. A good, clean wool blanket can be used under the pad. Keep it clean and dry.

Bell

Feed Bag

Hobbles

Chain Type

This type is rugged and hard for an animal to slip out of. It also can be fastened together with a bull snap and double as a single foot picket hobble.

Utah or Double Ring

This one is available in nylon, as well as leather. Nylon does not stretch when wet. It may be buckled around horse's neck for carrying.

Single Hobble

This hobble can be used for staking out.

Gunnysack

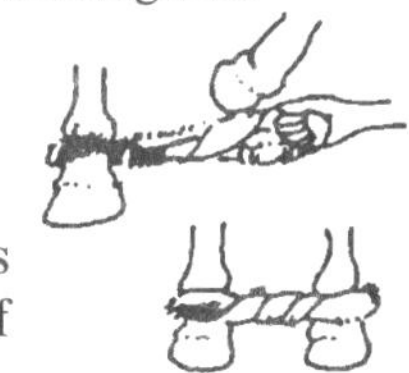

This homemade hobble works well. Cut about 6" to 8" out of the top of a gunnysack.

Lash Rope and Cinch

Use a 45' lash rope so it will be long enough to tie the double diamond. It may be made of cotton or nylon and should be 1/2" diameter. Other small 3/8" or 1/4" ropes can be used for manta ropes and slings. They can be 20' to 30' long, depending on use. My preference on lash ropes is the 1/2" three-strand, soft-spun nylon.

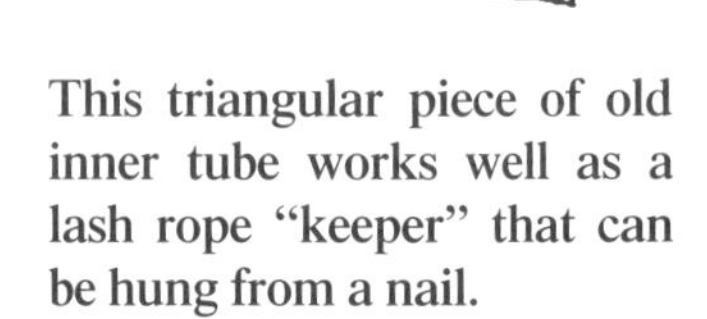

This triangular piece of old inner tube works well as a lash rope "keeper" that can be hung from a nail.

Here is a handy way to take care of your lash rope: Double the rope. Coil it, beginning with the cinch and loose end. When about 3' of rope remains, wrap it around the coiled rope 2 or 3 times and bring the loop end through the coiled rope and the cinch ring and hang the loop over a branch, a nail, saddlehorn or crossbuck. Real handy.

Sheepherder Stove

This stove has a telescoping stove pipe and removable screw-on legs. Both are stored in the stove's oven. Wrap in a gunnysack to reduce rattling.

Some of the new stoves fold up and are compact, but keep the hinges oiled!

Some stoves have an oven as well as a firebox. Others have only a firebox, and the oven is a separate unit that sits on top of the stove.

This homemade barrel stove shows the telescoping stove pipe. Stoves are handy. In summer, as well as in winter camps, to cook on, dry clothes on and take the chill off in a tent.

Duffle Bag

Pack personal gear, clothing or sleeping bag in a duffle bag to make loading up much easier.

The Manta and How to Use It

The manta is a piece of canvas, from 6' x 6' up to 10' x 12'. It is thrown over the load as a protective cover. Your gear will stay drier if you waterproof the manta. Don't use poly tarps or other rattly, noisy material or "old spook" may try to unload the pack before you are ready.

A manta may also be used to wrap up a bedroll, bale of hay, sack of grain, tent or any loose items to make them fit better in or on top of the pack. This is where a small 3/8" or 1/4" rope comes in handy to tie any type of bundle.

Fold the canvas around the bale as if gift-wrapping. With a honda in one end of the rope, make a loop and loop it over one end of the bale. Put two to three half hitches over the bale. Turn the bale over, run the loose rope end around the end of the bale and pass the rope around each loop around the bale. This will prevent the rope from slipping. Tie off at the original starting point where the honda is on the top side of bale.

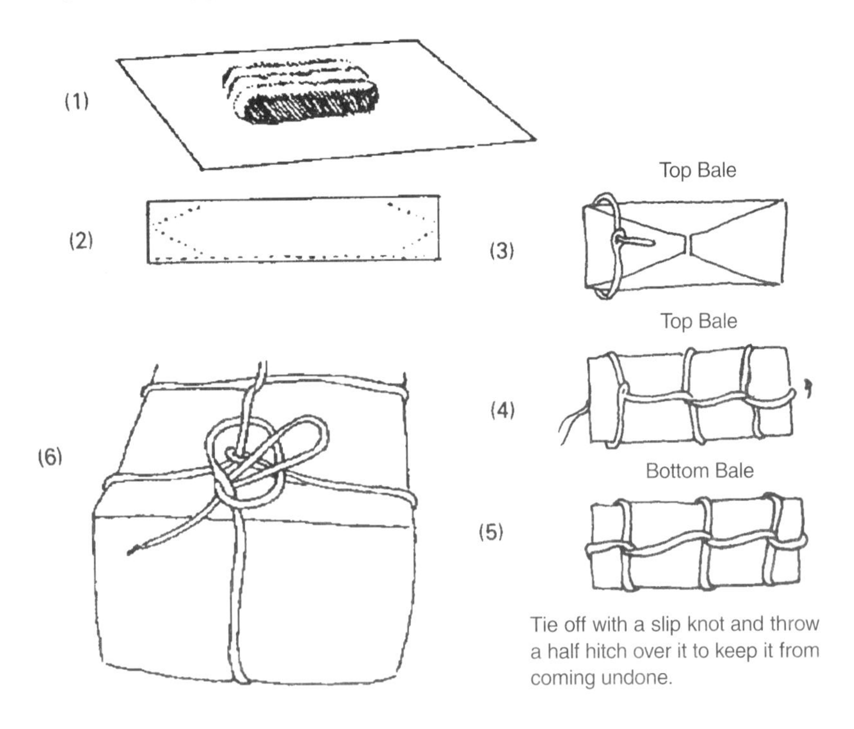

Packers in some parts of the country use all mantied packs and no panniers. They sling their loads on decker and crossbuck saddles.

Essential Equipment: Axe, Shovel, Bucket and Saw

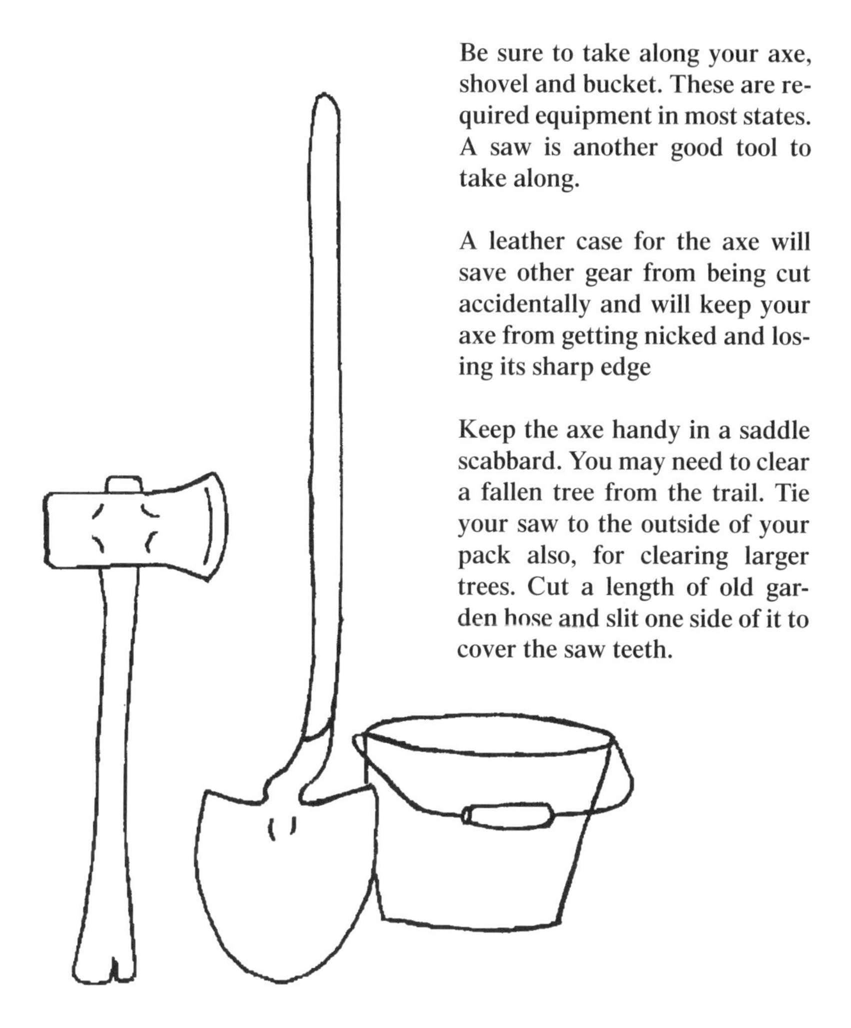

Be sure to take along your axe, shovel and bucket. These are required equipment in most states. A saw is another good tool to take along.

A leather case for the axe will save other gear from being cut accidentally and will keep your axe from getting nicked and losing its sharp edge

Keep the axe handy in a saddle scabbard. You may need to clear a fallen tree from the trail. Tie your saw to the outside of your pack also, for clearing larger trees. Cut a length of old garden hose and slit one side of it to cover the saw teeth.

LISTS AND WEIGHTS

CAMPING EQUIPMENT

Packer check list for ten people on a six-day summer trip. Check off before you leave.

Tents

Qty	Item	Approximate weight (pounds)
1	10' x 12' tent (3 people and cook tent)	30
36	Aluminum stakes (or cut your own)	8
1	Ridge pole (in small sections)	10
2	End poles (in small sections)	14
3	8' x 10' tents (3 people each)	76
93	Aluminum stakes (or cut your own)	16
3	Ridge poles (if needed for tent being used)	30
6	End poles (if needed)	42
	(Many tent poles and stakes are cut in camp, but some are packed in; a rope through the tent and tied to a tree at each end will also work.)	
	Total tent weight	226 lbs.

Camping Gear

Qty	Item	Weight
2	Sheepherder stoves with telescoping stove pipe	43
2	Portable camp toilets (or dig your own)	10
1	Folding camp shovel (wrapped in a gunnysack)	2
1	Single bit axe, with leather cover (can be packed in a scabbard); doubles as a hammer	3
2	Battery lanterns, 6-volt, and 1 extra battery (gas or butane lanterns can also be used)	4
1	Large caliber rifle on guide's horse	
1	.22-caliber revolver, on guide's or wrangler's horse; ammunition for rifle and revolver	2
	Charcoal briquets (optional)	10
1	Quart charcoal lighter (to start wet wood or briquets)	2
3	Collapsible water containers (to meet your needs)	1/2
1	Pair pliers, nails and hammer	
	Bailing wire comes in handy; pack in saddle bags	
1	2-way radio set or cell phone (might save a life; pack in saddle bags)	
	Total camping gear weight	76 1/2 lbs.

HORSE FEED

	Approximate weight (pounds)
Rolled oats or sweet feed for catching horses	50
Complete horse feed, 5/8" pellets (3 lbs./day/horse)	285
Grazing (half the string at a time)	
2 small salt blocks (2 at 4 lbs. each)	8
Total horse feed weight	343 lbs.

OTHER HORSE EQUIPMENT

Pack saddles, pads and panniers are not included in the weight list.

9	Mantas (10' x 12', 10 lbs. each)	90
16	Sets hobbles (approximately 1/2 lb. each)	8
6	Horseshoes, sizes: 0, 1, 2 (2 of each size)	6
	Horseshoe nails, packed in kitchen match box and taped shut, or Easyboots	1/2
4-5	Coils of 1/4" rope, 30' each (in saddle bags)	
1	Shoeing hammer (can double for other uses)	1/2
1	Pair hoof nippers	1/2
1	Hoof rasp	1/2
1	Hoof pick or knife	1/2
2	Metal currycombs	3
2	Rubber currycombs	5
4	Brushes (medium stiff)	1
24	Sheepskins (to help prevent galls and cinch sores)	1
	Total horse equipment weight	116 1/2 lbs.

COOKING EQUIPMENT

Utensils:	2	Skillets, 1-14", 1-12", cast iron	3
	2	Screen skillet covers	
	3	Pots, combination aluminum set, 3 1/2, 2 1/2, 1 1/2 qt.	2
	2	Dishpans, metal	4
	2	Coffee pots	3
	2	Biscuit pans	2
	3	Wash pans, metal	2

Category	Qty	Item	Approximate weight (pounds)
	2	Over fire grates	2
	1	Aluminum grill	2
	3	Mixing bowls and 1 baking pan	1
	1	Dutch oven, large size aluminum	5
Silverware:	1	Dipper	1
	12	Each: forks, knives, spoons (in canvas holder)	1
	6	Large serving spoons, 3 cooking forks	1/2
		Sharp knife in leather case	1/2
Dishes:	12	Plates - durable plastic - (use paper products if you prefer and don't like to do dishes)	4
	12	Bowls	3
	12	Cups	3
Other:	2	Spatulas, 1 large, 1 small	1/2
	2	Can openers	1/2
		Kitchen matches soaked in wax and stored in water proof container	
	3	Plastic quart bottles with wide mouth	1
	3	Plastic jars, pint size	2
	12	Plastic sealable bags (for packing, storage and use as fish bags)	
	1	Gallon plastic jar for eggs (break eggs into jar is another idea for packing eggs)	1
	4	Hard plastic egg containers	2
	80	Baggies for sandwiches and leftovers	1
	12	Dishtowels (also used in packing)	1
	4	Handtowels	1/2
	12	Dishrags	1/2
	2	Scouring pads	1/2
	10	Trash bags, plastic heavy duty (pack it in-pack it out)	1
	1	Aluminum foil, heavy duty roll	3
	1	Liquid dishwashing soap (biodegradable)	1
	4	Potholders	1/2
		Napkins, 160 family pack (10 persons, 16 meals)	1
	3	Large rolls of paper towels, heavy duty (wrap in plastic bag to keep dry, also use in packing)	1
Total cooking equipment			57 lbs.

FIRST AID SUPPLIES

Human First Aid Kit

Put first aid supplies in a sturdy container to withstand the knocks of a high mountain trip. Use plastic containers rather than glass. This list sounds like a lot, but these supplies may help make your trip more pleasant and safe. You never know what will happen next. Replenish after each trip, and store the kit in the house over the winter so items do not freeze.

Milk of Magnesia tablets
First aid cream
Butterfly Band-Aids
Adhesive tape
2-40" triangular bandages
Small bottle rubbing alcohol
Needle (for sewing)
Razor blades
Scissors
Safety pins (large and small)
Matches (strike-anywhere type)
Water purification tablets
Phenomint gum
Kaopectate
Tums and Pepto Bismol
Mercurochrome
Insect repellent
Aspirin, Advil, Tylenol or
Aleve (take a variety)
Band-Aids, preferably 1"
3 compresses
6-3" x 3" sterile gauze compresses
3" Ace bandage
Stretch gauze
Cold tablets
Thread
Tweezers
Murine
Hand soap
Small candle
Snakebite kit
Burn ointment
Toothache kit
Universal antidote
Suntan lotion
Dark glasses (if needed)

Total weight for human first aid kit 11 lbs.

Water purification tips: This is of utmost importance, wherever you go. Don't take a chance. You might get Giardia or other parasities. Here are a few ideas:

1. Boil drinking water at least 30 minutes.
2. Use water purification tablets.
3. Use the special drinking straws.
4. Various filters are also good.
5. Water treatment kits are a must and well worth the cost.

Possible accidents or illnesses connected with a pack trip:

- Thrown from a horse
- Kicked by a horse
- Punctures and abrasions
- Broken bones
- Nose bleeds
- Wood ticks
- Lightning strike
- Muscle cramps
- Hangover
- Food poisoning (fire the cook)
- Altitude sickness
- Heart attack or stroke
- Bee/wasp/mosquito bites
- Toe stepped on
- Sprains
- Splinters
- Lacerations
- Wounds caused by rusty items
- Eye injuries
- Bites and stings
- Fish hook injuries
- Shock
- Poisonous plants
- Rope burns
- Hypothermia

Prescriptions: Keep prescription medication on your person or in your saddle bags and be sure others know how to administer them to you in an emergency. Write down the instructions and give them to the person in charge.

Horse First Aid Kit

Supplies: Increase bandage materials for each additional horse

- 4 rolls 3" Elasticon
- Duct tape
- 6 rolls 3" gauze
- 1 package 3"x 3" gauze sponges
- 3 disposable diapers
- Surgical scissors
- Disposable surgical blades
- 1 roll cotton
- Screwdriver, pliers
- Surgical soap (Betadyne, Nolvasan)
- Surgical solution (Betadyne, Nolvasan)
- Opthalmic antibiotic eye ointment
- Hoof knife
- 1 pair mosquito forceps (hemostat)
- 3 rolls Vetrap
- Disposable razor
- 1 roll 2" white tape
- Betadyne (tamed Iodine)
- Tetanus toxoid vaccine, 2 doses (keep cold)
- Procaine G penicillin, 100cc bottle (keep cold)
- Rompun (tranquilizer, analgesic)
- Dexamethazone injectable
- Azium (steriod powder)
- Nitrofurazone ointment
- Icthymal ointment (drawing agent)
- Easy boots and Velcro keepers
- 8 3/8" x no. 8 sheet metal screws
- 8 flat washers
- 4 20cc disposable syringes
- 4 12cc disposable syringes
- 20 18g x 1 1/2" needles
- Sterile saline solution
- Mastitis ointment
- Phenylbutazone paste (1 tube)
- Sulfa powder
- Banamine injectable

The supplies listed above should be packed tightly in a suitable metal or hard plastic container. Paper towels are always useful and may be packed around the supplies to prevent damage on the trail. Your emergency kit will enable you to administer first aid for most problems that you may encounter on the trail. Every effort, however, should be made to obtain professional help at the earliest possible time. There is a great potential for serious permanent damage to your animal in the event that you make an improper diagnosis and render an inadequate or incorrect treatment. Your local veterinarian can supply you with most of these items or their equivalent. Consider his or her recommendations and be sure you understand and can perform the following treatments.

General Considerations

When an emergency occurs, keep calm and take your time. Horses are especially prone to react negatively to your anxiety. A few minutes spent talking quietly with your patient prior to giving any treatment will help alleviate his apprehension and substantially reduce the total time required for the treatment.

Preconditioning

Prepare your animals at home prior to the trip. A 10 to 30-day conditioning program, using the equipment that you plan to pack with, will allow you to make all adjustments and condition the animals. Make sure that the animals are properly shod one to two weeks prior to departure. The horse's digesitve system will not readily tolerate changes in feedstuffs or in feeding schedules. Plan to start grazing your animals on grass for short periods of time during this preconditioning program if you are planning to let them graze for their roughage while on the trip. Allow sufficient time to thoroughly train your animals to the hobbles or tether rope before starting into the wilderness. It is a good idea to allow your animals to "camp out" in your back yard for several nights during the preconditioning program. Riding or ponying your animals for 6 to 10 miles per week to toughen up their backs, muscles and legs will aid greatly. Numerous sacking-out experiences may be needed for younger stock to get them used to packs and pack ropes.

All injectable medications listed should be administered by means of an 18g x 1 1/2" needle. Insert the needle, with a quick thrust, deep into the muscles of the neck or rear leg (as demonstrated to you by your veterinarian prior to the trip). If blood should appear in the needle, withdraw it and reinsert it at another location. After the needle has been placed, attach the syringe and inject the medication slowly. Do not inject these medications directly into a blood vessel.

Keep all of your supplies and equipment clean at all times. All disposable items should be discarded after use. Discard and replace all medications in accordance with the expiration date on the container. Penicillin and tetanus toxoid should be kept as cool as possible and should be replaced at the start of each trip. All other supplies should remain stable until their respective expiration dates.

Possible Problems and Treatments

Cinch Galls and Saddle Sores

Description: These lesions will vary from a warm, raised plaque to a raw bleeding ulcer. All lesions of this type are caused by improper adjustment, poor fit, dirty equipment, poor conditioning or a combination of all.

Prevention: When you arrive in camp, readjust or remove the saddle and allow air to circulate under the blankets. After the weight is removed, retighten the cinch to a snug position. Allow 30 to 45 minutes for the back to cool down and gradually adjust to the reduced weight load before finally removing the saddle for the night. Re-examine the back and cinch area one to two hours later for any warm or raised areas.

Treatment: Apply cold packs directly to the warm or raised area and resaddle over the cold pack to keep pressure on the lesion. Continue to check and replace the cold packs until all swelling is gone. These raised areas will become raw after the next ride unless they are properly treated. Raw areas should be treated with cold packs and pressure, followed by a light covering of an anitbiotic salve. Readjust your equipment or cut a hole in the saddle pad to prevent further contact with the galled area.

Rope Burns

Description: Most rope burns occur on the back of the hind pastern area. These may become painful if neglected.

Treatment: Thoroughly scrub the affected area with surgical soap. Cut the hair away from the wound and rinse thoroughly. Allow the hoof wall and hair to dry completely before applying a bandage. Mix four parts Nitrofurazone antibiotic ointment with one part Azium powder. Mix this preparation thoroughly and saturate an unfolded gauze sponge with the medication. Gently apply the medicated sponge to the rope burned area. Wrap the 3" Vetrap or Elasticon tightly around the hoof wall, coming under the heels. Continue to wrap tightly up to and around the fetlock. An Easyboot placed over the shoe and bandaged hoof will protect the bandage for several days. It is important to protect the burned area from all moisture. Administer 20cc Procaine G penicillin to a 1,000-pound horse once a day for five days. The animal should warm out of any lameness in 15 to 30 minutes of exercise.

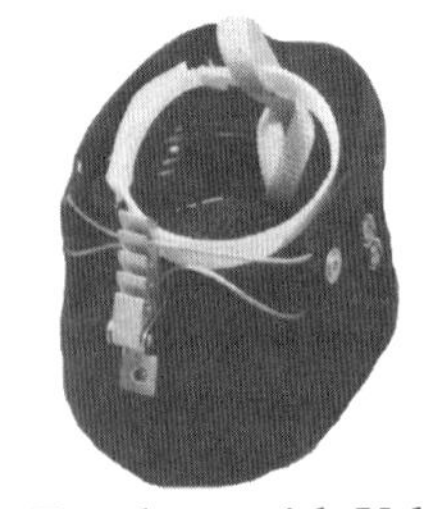

Easyboot with Velcro keeper to put around fetlock so you don't lose it in a boggy area.

Stonebruises and Foot Punctures

Description: Sharp stones, sticks and other pointed objects may either seriously bruise or puncture the sole or frog area. Strong pressure with a blunt object should provoke a pain reaction and will enable you to localize the injured area. Clean the sole with the hoof knife, paring away suspicious areas to determine if penetration has occurred.

Treatment: Leave the shoe on the foot to keep the sole elevated. An Easyboot placed over the shoe will provide adequate protection for simple bruises. Penetrating wounds should be excavated thoroughly with a hoof knife to provide drainage and then flushed with Betadyne. Place gauze soaked with Betadyne over the hole and secure the pack with Elasitcon. Cover the hoof with an Easyboot. The Betadyne pack should be changed daily. Extreme caution should be used to prevent water and mud from packing into the wound. Administer 20cc Procaine G penicillin per day for five days. If the Easyboots are going to be used for further riding, a pair of no. 8 x 3/8" screws placed in the hoof wall will prevent loss in boggy and rocky country.

Lacerations

Description: Generally lacerations of muscled areas do not present the potential for permanent damage that can occur with lacerations of the lower leg, especially when a joint capsule has been involved. Blood loss, although quite traumatic to humans, is seldom a serious problem unless a major artery has been severed.

Treatment: Thoroughly cleanse the wound with surgical soap. Use the soap as a lather and shave the hair from the margins of the wound. Rinse the wound with diluted surgical solution. Rinse thoroughly with sterile saline and apply a thin layer of Nitrofurazone ointment. Give one dose tetanus toxoid vaccine. Administer 20cc Procaine G penicillin once a day for five to seven days and Phenylbutazone paste at 2 grams per day. Wounds on the body or upper leg cannot be bandaged, but wounds on the lower legs should be bandaged until veterinary help is sought. Bandaging below the knee is easy if you take the time to have your veterinarian show you how. Failure to bandage properly does more harm than no bandage at all. After cleansing the wound and clipping the hair, dry the part of the limb that will be under the bandage. Apply a sterile telfa pad or diaper directly to the wound. Secure this with a roll of gauze wrapped snugly enough to keep the telfa or diaper in place. Avoid wrapping too tightly.

Next, apply roll cotton, starting at the hoof and circling upward to 5" above the wound. Secure the cotton by using a roll of gauze and repeating the path from the hoof upward. This can be done fairly tightly. Next, repeat the same step using Vetrap. Elasticon can be used by putting one circle around the hoof and one around the top of the bandage. One of the keys to bandaging is to put even pressure from top to bottom and always cover the bulbs of the heel. For example, if you can see the pastern, start over! Any swelling above or below the bandage means you need to change it immediately. Change bandages every two days.

Description: These lesions may involve the eye itself or the surrounding areas. Any scratch or laceration on the eyeball is a potentially serious condition and should receive professional care as soon as possible. A few hours can mean the difference between losing eyesight or not.

Treatment: Great patience may be required to examine and treat the horse's eye. Gently flush the eye with warm physiologic saline and examine for any foreign bodies. Carefully examine the shiny portion of the eyeball for any defect. Gently apply small amounts of an opthalmic antibiotic ointment for eyes, at four-hour intervals. Be sure the ointment does not have any steriod content. If there is any damage to the cornea, steriods will worsen the damage. Keep horse away from light, dust and wind. Administer Phenylbutazone paste at 2 grams per 1,000-pound horse, per day, orally.

Insect Bites

Description: Most insect bites are classified as an inconvenience, although some may cause a rather severe reaction. Single or multiple swellings usually occur on the animal's skin. Most insect bite reactions subside within 12 hours.

Treatment: Cold packs placed over local swelling will suffice for most bites. Serious reactions may be treated with 2-4 grams Phenylbutazone paste orally per 1,000-pound horse and/or 5cc Banamine per 1,000-pound horse intramuscularly.

Snakebites

Description: Most snakebites occur on the horse's nose, probably as a result of excess curiosity. The head will swell to enormous proportions, possibly shutting down the airways.

Treatment: The animal should be transported to a veterinarian, if possible to do so without a great deal of stress to the patient. Administer 2cc Dexamethazone per 100 pounds. If breathing becomes a problem, give 2-4 grams Phenylbutazone paste orally and/or 15cc Banamine injection intramuscularly. Once the nose has become swollen a number of punctures (20-30) should be made with an 18g needle or with the end of a scalpel blade. Fluid will stream profusely from the puncture sites. Should the swelling continue and compromise the animal's respiration, the normal pink color of the gums will change to pinkish blue. At this point, an emergency tracheotomy may be necessary to save the animal's life. Shave an area 2" x 6" on the middle of the bottom portion of the neck one-third the distance between the throatlash and the chest. Scrub the area with surgical soap and rinse with surgical solution. You should be able to feel the cartilage of the tracheal ring just under the skin. Make a quick incision through the skin and into the trachea. A 20cc disposable syringe that has been cut off at the 5 cc mark and inserted through the skin and into the trachea will serve as a temporary airway. This procedure should obviously not be attempted except as a last resort.

Abdominal Pain (Colic)

Description: An abdominal crisis may be accompanied by any combination of the classic signs of colic. It is obviously impossible for the lay person to differentiate between the many forms of the syndrome or to make an accurate diagnosis. A general treatment has been outlined that might well be contradicted if the correct diagnosis were known. It is felt, however, that this treatment will ultimately save more animals than it will harm. The signs of colic include but are not limited to:

Decreased appetite	Increased abdominal sounds
Anxious expression	Looking at flank area
Sweating, pawing	Rapid pulse and respiration
Rolling	Kicking at belly

Treatment: Keep warm and walk **only** enough to prevent the animal from injuring itself. Allow the animal to lie down if it will do so without rolling. Administer 6cc Rompun to control pain. Horses can choke on Rompun, so give no food until it has worn off. Colic is life threatening. Seek help if the colic is severe or lasts more than an hour. In addition, give 15cc Banamine per 1,000-pound horse. Both Rompun and Banamine can be injected into the muscle.

Tying Up Syndrome (Azoturia)

Description: This condition is commonly seen shortly after a horse is started to be worked. The animal will refuse to move or will move with great difficulty. The muscles of the hindquarters will become stiff and hard. Many signs of colic may accompany this condition. When the animal urinates, the urine will be a dark brown, possibly with a reddish tint.

Treatment: Rest is imperative. Do not attempt to move the animal for about 12 hours (except into a horse trailer and to the vet). Keep the animal warm and supply water. Give 2 grams of Phenylbutazone paste every 12 hours. Give 2cc of Rompun. If the horse prefers to lie down, the prognosis is grave. Also give 15cc Banamine in the muscle.

Founder (Laminitis)

Description: Laminitis is characterized by moderate to extreme pain in the feet. The disease manifests itself primarily in the front feet of horses, although some cases may involve all four feet. Mules are rarely affected. The feet will become warm and a pounding pulse may be detected in the pastern area. The animal may stand with the forefeet extended as it strives to maintain its weight on the hind legs. It is imperative that the animal receive professional attention as quickly as possible. The difference of a few hours can drastically affect the eventual recovery.

Treatment: Move the animal to the softest ground possible (sand or mud). Administer 2cc Rompun per 1,000-pounds. Administer 2 grams Phenylbutazone paste every 12 hours.

PERSONAL GEAR

Pack in saddle bags:

- Camera and film
- Thermos, 1 pint
- Fishing creel and gear
- Snacks
- Small bar soap
- Cap with a bill
- Sunglasses
- Gloves
- Binoculars
- Matches (in waterproof container; use strike-anywhere kitchen matches)
- Medicines (if needed regularly)
- Toilet tissue (in plastic bag to keep dry)
- Lunch, when on trail
- Pliers and bailing wire

Tie on saddle:

Full-length slicker
Fishing rod (in steel case)
Warm coat
Canteen, with drinking water (purified/treated)

Carry on your person:

Sharp pocket knife
Licenses: fishing and/or hunting
Personal medication with instructions to administer

Pack in duffle bags (to go in panniers):

Shaving or cosmetic kit:

Toothpaste and brush
Hand cream
Soap
Suntan lotion
Hair comb or brush
Vaseline
Chapstick
Insect repellent

Clothing:

6 Pair of socks
Pajamas
1 Extra pair of boots
2-3 Shirts or blouses
2-3 Pair of underwear
2-3 Pair of jeans
Light overshoes
Sweater or sweatshirt
Long john underwear (for warmth and protection against saddle sores)

Pack in a stuff sack (separate from other personal gear):

Bedroll/sleeping bag
Air mattress or foam pad (you'll only forget it once)
Towels and washcloths
Night cap with ear flaps or a stocking cap (to keep head and ears warm)
Flashlight, new batteries
Air pump and repair kit
Light and heavy jacket
Pair of gloves
Deck of cards
Mink oil waterproofing

Critical items: Don't forget a first aid kit, map, compass and matches.

Personal gear weight limits:

15 lbs. per person	150
10 lbs. additional for fishermen (for 7)	70
10 lbs. sleeping bag and air mattress or foam pad	100

FOOD

Feed 'em well, treat 'em good and you'll have a great trip!

Menus

FIRST DAY

Lunch
- Roast beef sandwich, 2 each
- Pork and beans, individual can
- Fritos, small bag each
- Candy bar
- Beverage: coffee, tea, canned pop

Dinner
- Fried chicken (prepared earlier and heated in oven)
- Mashed potatoes (instant)
- Gravy mix
- Fresh cantaloupe
- Beverage: coffee, tea, canned drink

SECOND DAY

Breakfast
- Fried eggs, 2 each
- Hash browns, frozen
- Sausage links, 3 each
- Tomato juice
- Beverage: coffee, tea, hot chocolate

Lunch
- Ground round patty, 2 each
- Green beans
- Orange, fresh
- Beverage: coffee, tea, Kool-aid

Dinner
- T-bone steak and/or fresh fish (grilled, if any are caught)
- French fried potatoes, frozen
- Tossed salad, lettuce and tomato
- Canned pudding
- Beverage: coffee, tea, Kool-aid

Evening
- Popcorn: Tell a few stories and sing a few campfire songs

THIRD DAY

Breakfast
Pancakes, 4-5 each
Ham, canned
Orange juice
Beverage: coffee, tea, hot chocolate

Lunch
Sandwich, canned tuna fish
Carrot sticks (just like home)
Canned pears, individual can
Beverage: coffee, tea, Kool-aid

Dinner
Pork chops, 2 per person, grilled (watch for spoilage)
Whole kernel corn
Applesauce
Beverage: coffee, tea, Kool-aid
Smores around the camp fire

FOURTH DAY

Breakfast
Eggs, 3 per person, scrambled
Bacon
Sourdough biscuits
Apple juice
Beverage: coffee, hot chocolate

Lunch
Sandwich, canned meat
Vegetable soup, dried mix
Fresh apple (may be a little bruised)
Beverage: coffee, tea, Kool-aid

Fourth Day cont.

Dinner
Baked ham, canned
Baked beans
Yams
Brownies, mix
Beverage: coffee, tea, Kool-aid

FIFTH DAY

Breakfast
French toast, 4 slices each
Bacon
Grapefruit sections, canned
Beverage: coffee, tea, hot chocolate

Lunch
Chili: Easy on the beans! (For those with stomach problems, offer a milder soup as an alternative.)
Beef tamales
Applesauce
Beverage: Coffee, tea Kool-aid

Dinner
Chicken and dumplings, canned or fresh fish
Carrots, canned
Fruit cocktail
Beverage: coffee, tea, Kool-aid

Evening
Marshmallow roast and hot chocolate. Swap some stories!

SIXTH DAY

Breakfast
Pancakes (sourdough if you wish)
Fried ham, canned
Grape juice
Beverage: coffee, tea, hot chocolate

Lunch
Will be brought from the ranch to meet the folks at the end of the trail!
Fried chicken or hamburgers
Potato salad
Tossed salad
Baked beans
Beverage: coffee, canned pop

OFFERED AT ALL MEALS

Bread	Margarine
Salt and pepper	Jelly
Coffee creamer	Sugar
Mustard	Ketchup
Syrup	

EXTRA MENUS: Plan and pack grub for one extra day in case you get snowed in or stranded. Try not to take heavy items, because you may not need them.

Breakfast
Spam
Pancakes
Beverage: coffee, tea, hot chocolate

Lunch
Spaghetti and meatballs, canned
Yellow wax beans
Apricots, canned
Beverage: coffee, tea, Kool-aid

Dinner
Beef stew
Peas, canned
Peaches, canned
Beverage: coffee, tea, Kool-aid

Menu Options: Depending on your preferences, diets and weight factor, you can modify with freeze-dried foods or cut back on amounts served and adjust to fit your situation.

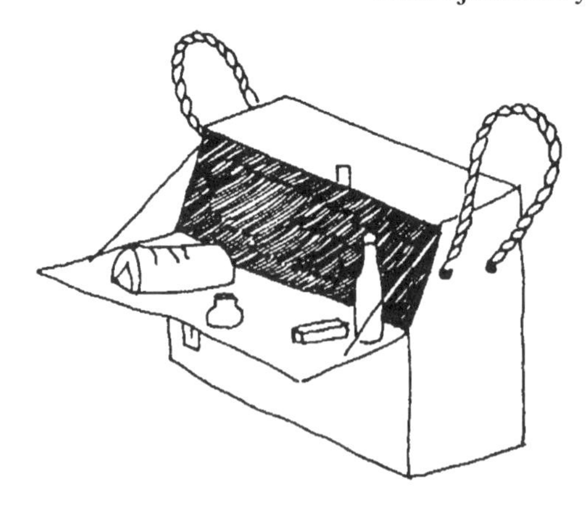

Recipes

Sourdough (Sansom)

Make the starter before your trip. Place 1 cup milk in a glass or plastic jar (no metal) and allow to stand at room temperature for 24 hours. Stir in 1 cup flour. To speed process, cover jar with cheese cloth and place outside for several hours to expose dough to the wild yeast cells floating in the winds. Leave uncovered in a warm place (80°F is ideal) for two to five days, depending on how long it takes to bubble and sour. A good place is near the pilot light on a gas range or in any moderately warm place. Do not place it too close to the pilot light. Too much heat will kill the yeast. If it starts to dry out, stir in enough tepid water to bring it back to the original consistency. Once it has a good sour aroma and it's full of bubbles, it's ready to use.

Try to maintain about 1 1/2 cups starter

Each time you use part of your starter, replenish it with a mixture of equal amounts of milk and flour. Leave at room temperature several hours or overnight or until it again becomes full of bubbles; then cover and store it in the refrigerator.

Use at least once a week

The starter is best if you use it at least once a week. If you do not use it for two or three weeks, spoon out and discard about half of the starter and replenish it as described above. Given good care, a starter becomes more flavorful with age. If you don't plan to use the starter for several weeks or more, it is a good idea to freeze it to slow down the yeast action. If frozen leave it at room temperature for 24 hours after thawing and before using.

Once you have your starter and use it frequently, you'll get to know it as an old friend. You'll know how to control the sourness to suit your own taste, as well as how long it will take to act (rise) in the recipes you make throughout the year. It works faster in warmer months.

Sourdough Pancakes (Kaltenbach)

Mix starter with 3 cups flour and 3 cups milk. Allow to stand overnight. The next morning mix, remove and save 1/2 cup starter. Add 2 eggs, 1 tablespoon sugar, 1 teaspoon salt, 1 tablespoon cooking oil. Mix. Add 1 heaping teaspoon baking soda slowly while stirring. Allow to stand for a few minutes. Cook and enjoy.

Sourdough Recipes

With an active starter you can make pancakes, waffles, biscuits, hot rolls, cornbread and a variety of other breads. You learn to understand variables as you work with sourdough. A double leavening action from the yeast action in the starter exists in all sourdough recipes. The more sour the starter, the more soda you must add. Begin by using the suggested amount, based on average sourness. With experience you can judge the proper amount. Don't increase or decrease it more than 50 percent. You will also find that the rising times will vary with temperature. The cooler it is, the longer you allow. **Never add soda to your starter. It kills the yeast.**

Cocoa Mix

1 8-oz. creamer (if desired)
1 lb. can of chocolate (Hershey's or Nestle's Quick)
1 lb. powdered sugar
10 2/3 cups (medium size box) powdered milk

Stir thoroughly in a large container. Use 1/4 to 1/2 cup of this mixture per cup of beverage and add hot water. Store in a plastic jar.

EASY TO PACK. EASY TO MAKE.

Food List

Pack trips sure do work up an appetite!

B - breakfast L - lunch D - dinner

(See p. 44 for hints and tips on packing food.)

Bacon	5 lbs.	2B	1 lb. per 4 people	5
Chicken	3 fryers	1D	1 lb. per 3 people	9
Sausage, frozen	3 lbs.	1B	1 lb. per 4 people	3
T-bone steak, frozen	10 steaks	1D	1 1/4 lbs. each	13
Ground round, frozen	5 lbs.	1L	1/2 lb. each	5
Pork chops, frozen	20 chops	1D	1-2 per person	10
Canned chicken	3 cans, 52 oz.	1D		9
Canned meat	4 cans, 12 oz.	2L		3
Canned ham	3 cans, 5 lbs.	2B, 1D		15
Beef stew	3 cans, 1 1/2 lbs.	1D		4
Tuna fish	4 cans, 12 1/2 oz.	1L		3
Eggs (grade AA large)	5 doz.	2B		8
				87 lbs.

Vegetables

Peas	3 cans	1D	1 can for 3 persons	3
Potatoes, instant	1 box	1D		1
Green beans	3 cans	1L	1-lb. can	3
Yellow wax beans	3 cans	1L	1-lb. can	3
Carrots	3 cans	1D	1-lb. can	3
Whole kernel corn	3 cans	1D	1-lb. can	3
Yams	1 can, 40 oz.	1D		3
Pork and beans	10 cans, 8 oz.	1L	1 can for each, in saddle bag	
Baked beans	2 cans, 30 oz.	1D		4
Dried soup	3 boxes	1L		1
Onions, fresh	4			2
Lettuce, fresh	2 heads	1D		2
Tomatoes, fresh	3	1D		1
Carrots, fresh	12	1L		2
Hash browns, frozen	4 boxes	1B		4
French fries, frozen	3 boxes	1D		3
				38 lbs.

Fruit

	Quantity	*Meals*	*Serving*	*Weight*
Applesauce	6 cans	1L, 1D	1 can for 3 persons	6
Grapefruit	3 cans	1B	1-lb. can	3
Peaches	3 cans	1D	1-lb. can	3
Apricots	3 cans	1L	1-lb. can	3
Pears	3 cans	1L	1-lb. can	3
Fruit cocktail	3 cans	1D	1-lb. can	3
Oranges, fresh	10	1L		3
Apples, fresh	10	1L		3
Cantaloupe, fresh	3	1D		6
				33 lbs.

Bread and Cereal Group

Bread, 6 slices/person/day (for sandwiches and French toast)	12 loaves			15
Brownie mix	2 boxes	1D		1
Bisquick, for pancakes, to flour fish, biscuits, bread (if needed), dumplings or use sourdough recipe (if you use the sourdough, take some flour and powdered milk to replenish the starter)	2 boxes			5
				21 lbs.

Beverages

Coffee (don't forget)	1 can	Every meal, 50 cups/lb.		3
Tea bags	1 box	Most meals		1/2
Canned pop	20 cans	2 L, in saddle bags		
Kool-aid	10 pkgs.	6 meals		1/2
Powdered milk	1 box, 38 oz.			2
Creamer (for coffee)	Container			4
Chocolate drink mix	1 can, 32 oz.	7 meals		2
Apple juice	1 can, qt.	1		1
Tomato juice	1 can, qt.	1		1
Orange juice	2 cans, qt.	2		2
Grape juice	2 cans, qt.	2		2
				18 lbs.

	Quantity	Meals	Serving	Weight
Sweets				
Smores fixings	1 box Graham crackers			1
	10 Hershey chocolate bars			1
	marshmallows, 1 bag			1
Candy bars	5, 6-packs			2
Caramel squares	1 bag			1
Jelly	2 jars, 10 oz.			1
Syrup	1 bottle, 24 oz.			2
				9 lbs.

Other Food Items

Pudding	10 cans	1D	4-5 oz.	3
Chili	2 cans	1L	20 oz.	5
Tamales	1 can	1L	29 oz.	2
Spaghetti and meat balls	2 cans	1L	20 oz.	5
Popcorn (a fun luxury)	1 can	Party		1
Gravy mix	4 boxes	1L		1
French toast mix, dried	1 box	1B		1
				18 lbs.

Condiments

Margarine	2 lbs. +	All meals	2
Shortening	1 lb. can	" "	1
Salt		" "	1/2
Pepper		" "	
Ketchup	2 bottles, 20 oz.	" "	2
Mustard	1 bottle, 5 oz.	" "	1/2
Sugar	1 sack	" "	3
Mayonnaise, low fat (Caution: Must keep cool)	3 jars, 8 oz.	" "	1
			10 lbs.

Total weight of all food items	235 lbs.

THE WEIGHT FACTOR

Weight Summary - Equipment and Supplies

	Weight
Camping equipment:	
Tents	226
Camping gear	76 1/2
Cooking equipment	57
First-Aid supplies	11
Horse:	
Feed	343
Equipment	116 1/2
First-Aid supplies	2
Personal gear:	
15 lb. per person, 10 people	150
10 lb. per fisherman or hunter, 7 people	70
10 lb. sleeping bags, foam pads or air mattresses	100
Food:	235
Total estimated weight for all 10 pack horses	1,387 lbs.

Pannier Balance and Weights

It is critical that the load be balanced and that each pannier weigh the same. Weigh and check each of them!

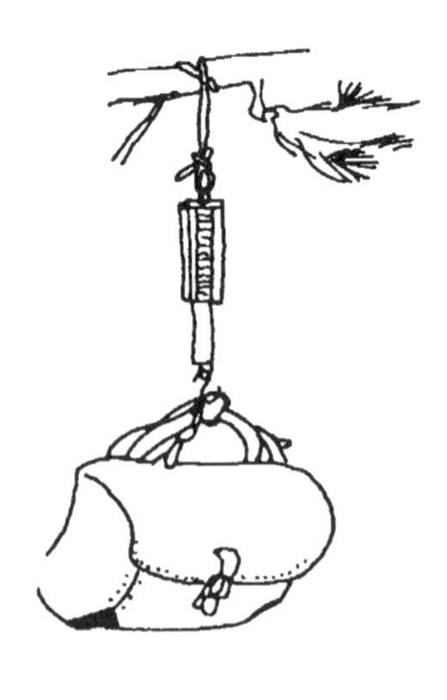

PACK HORSES NEEDED

Use 10 pack horses for the 1,387 pounds. **A horse can carry about 12.5 percent of his body weight** (excluding weight of saddle, panniers and pads). The pack string includes the following:

Pack animals	Weight	Load with	Total
2	1,200	150	= 300 lbs.
7	1,100	138	= 966 lbs.
1	1,000	121	= 121 lbs.
		Total	= 1,387 lbs

Bulky items, such as bedrolls and bread, should be distributed evenly on the loads. Each pannier should be weighed to assure uniform and balanced loads.

Mules and burros can be packed with up to 15 percent of their body weight if the load is well balanced and secure.

Clipping in Early Spring

Because mules and burros take longer to shed their winter coats, you may need to clip them if you plan to use them early in the summer. This will prevent hair balls and overheating.

Remember that pack animals' backs are more tender in the spring due to inactivity during the winter months. Preconditioning is important.

PACKING UP

A few tips and hints

Eggs:	1. Use the hard plastic egg containers lined with paper towels to help cushion the eggs, or wrap each in a baggie. Paper towels are handy, too, for cleaning up if eggs get broken. 2. Or, break all the eggs into a clean, plastic jar and seal tight. (Keep cool!) 3. Or, leave eggs in their original carton and pack cartons where they will not get crunched.
Glassware:	Avoid taking jars if possible. For those you must take, wrap them in newspapers, paper towels or dish towels, and put them in a protected place in the panniers.
Frozen foods:	Wrap in heavy newspaper and put in a plastic bag. Store in a shady, cool place in camp. Use up fresh meat in the first three days (watch it closely). Insulated bags and panniers are helpful.
Bedroll or sleeping bag:	Wrap in a canvas manta, stuff sack or duffle bag. Pack on top of the panniers and secure with the strap that goes over the top from one pannier to the other.
Tents:	Can be used as mantas or spread over the pack and covered by a manta. Some can be stuffed in a pannier. Tent poles, if packed, should be put in a manta and tied tight to prevent wear, rattling and losing them along the trail.
Personal gear:	Use a duffle bag for clothes and other personal items. Dry clothes and footwear can feel good at times, so pack in a plastic bag.
Newspapers:	Use for packing, for under cots, to insulate frozen foods and to start fires.
Fishing rods:	The short (18” to 24”) steel cases are best to protect your rod. If you have no case, tie your rod to a stick of the same length, pack in a pannier corner or tie on top and hope for the best.
Axe:	Use a leather cover for the axe head and place in a saddle scabbard on saddle horse.
Bucket:	Tie on top to the hitch rope.
Shovel:	A short handled shovel is easy to put in a pannier or tie outside to the hitch rope.

PACK ANIMAL SPEED INDEX

Normal speed: Your pack animal takes two steps per four seconds slower than the horse you're riding. One attempted mouthful of grass every 11 steps.

2nd gear: He passes your saddle horse on either side every 62 feet. Needs to be slapped with rope but will pull back when you do and jerk you out of saddle. Eats grass at a trot. Ducks lead rope under your saddle horse's tail every 600 feet. Results: Two wrecks per mile.

3rd gear: Likes to walk ahead of lead horse by at least two feet. Goes on wrong side of most trees. Catches your horse's rump (or your leg) on pannier. Your temptation to turn pack horse loose is strong. Don't do that. Your supper is in those packs.

4th gear: You turned him loose. Eddie Arcaro aboard Secretariate couldn't keep him in sight on a fast track. If you can head him off, he'll run off into the timber. If you can't, you'll be running an ad in the newspaper.

5th gear: He saw a bear and sold the farm. In rough country this situation is worse, because he gains speed jumping logs. Shoot him if you can (the horse, not the bear).

Author unknown. Thanks for the realistic trail humor!

CHAPTER 2

Rope Terminology

Terms
Types

ROPE TERMS

Used in Handling and Tying Rope

Running End	The end of the rope with which you are working when you tie a knot.
Standing End	The inactive length of the rope or end that is tied to something.
The Bight	A bend or U-shaped curve in the rope.
Overhand Loop	Made by crossing the end over the standing part.
Underhand Loop	Made by crossing the end under the standing part.
Turn	Taken by looping the rope around an object (often another section of itself).
Drawing Up	Once formed, a knot must be drawn up, or tightened slowly and evenly, to make certain that all sections of the knot arrangement keep their place and shape. Quick or careless tightening may result in a useless tangle.

ROPE TYPES

Natural Fiber Rope	**Manila** fiber makes the best and strongest natural fiber rope. **Sisal** fiber rope is 75 to 80% as strong as manila and is less flexible but more resistant to abrasion. **Cotton** fiber rope is used for packaging, clotheslines and sash cords, but is not satisfactory for general packing. Soft cotton is good for tying up a horse's foot or for a staking rope.

Synthetic Fiber Rope Synthetic fiber rope made from **nylon** or **dacron** is stronger than manila rope. It is especially useful under wet conditions, because the fibers do not absorb water and are not damaged by rot or mildew. Such rope is best adapted for use as towlines, starter ropes and lariats. **Polypropylene** rope is also used, but most has a slick, hard finish, that will cause rope burns easily and tends to "ball up." **Polyethylene** rope, being lighter than water, will float.

There is a wide variety of rope materials, construction and uses.

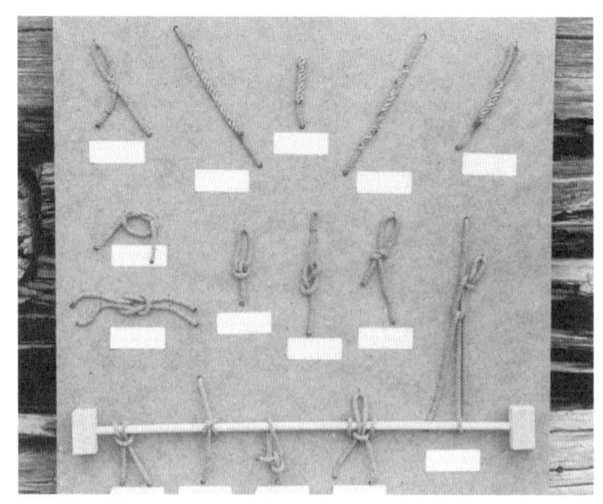

I recommend the 3-strand, 1/2" soft spun nylon. Soft cotton works well for tying up a foot. But for lead ropes and lash ropes, nylon is hard to beat.

High Country Wildlife

Wildlife is abundant in the high country. Gary Keimig's art shows the majesty of the bull elk. Mule deer, white tail deer, grouse, chipmonks and many other game and non-game species can be seen in the back country. Binoculars and cameras can help you take home many wildlife memories of your next pack trip.

CHAPTER 3

Hitches

Single Diamond
Half Diamond
Squaw Hitch
Double Diamond
Arizona or Basket Hitch
Basket Sling
Barrel Sling
Tying Off a Hitch
Tying on a Sheepherder Stove and a Bucket
Packing Meat

HITCHES

Single Diamond

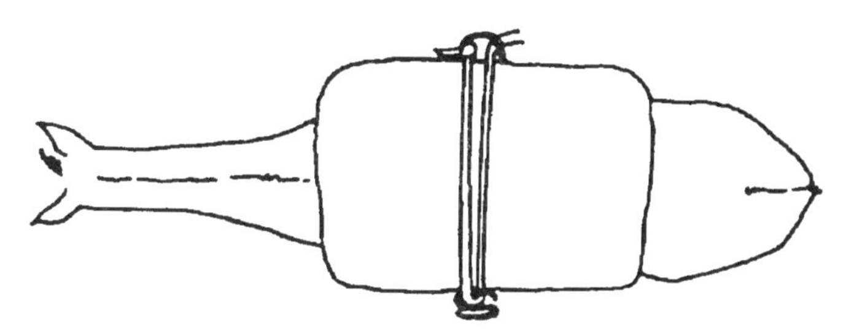

The near side partner always takes the right rope over the left!

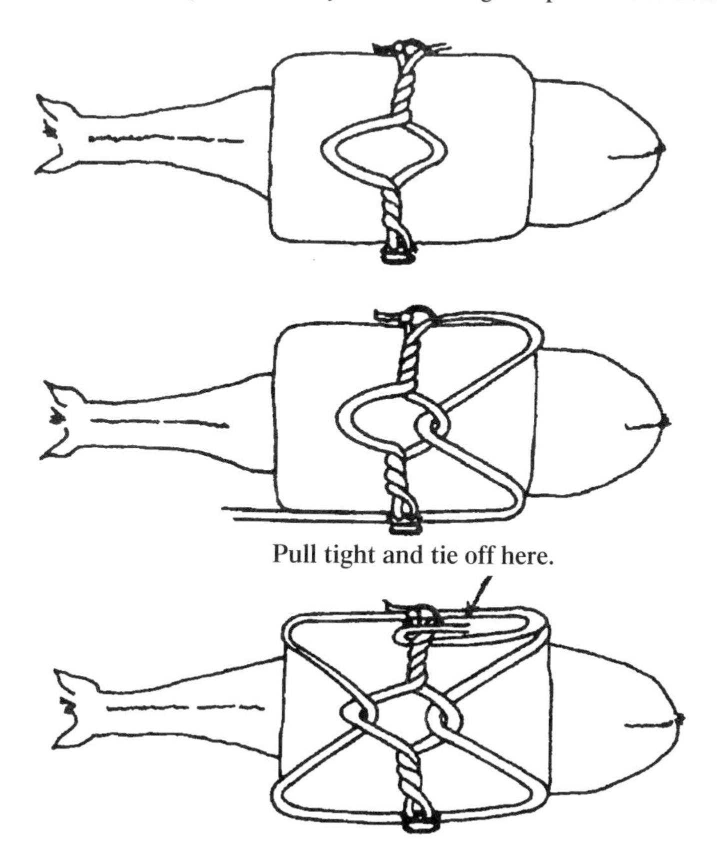

Half Diamond

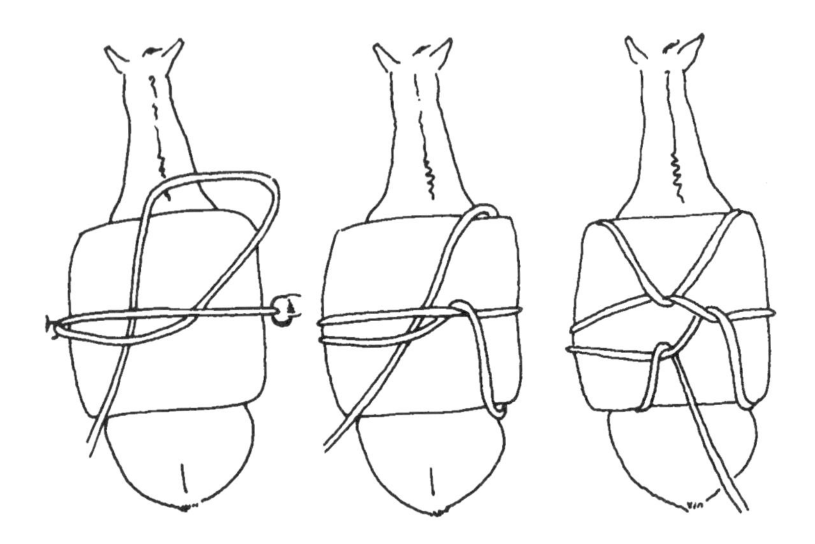

This hitch is not used a great deal, but it does require less rope than some other hitches.

Here's an easy way to hold your rope tight as you tie a hitch by yourself.

Be sure your hitch is tight before you tie off, or your entire hitch will be loose.

Don't use this on the double diamond, as the ropes need to slip and adjust.

Running end

Squaw Hitch

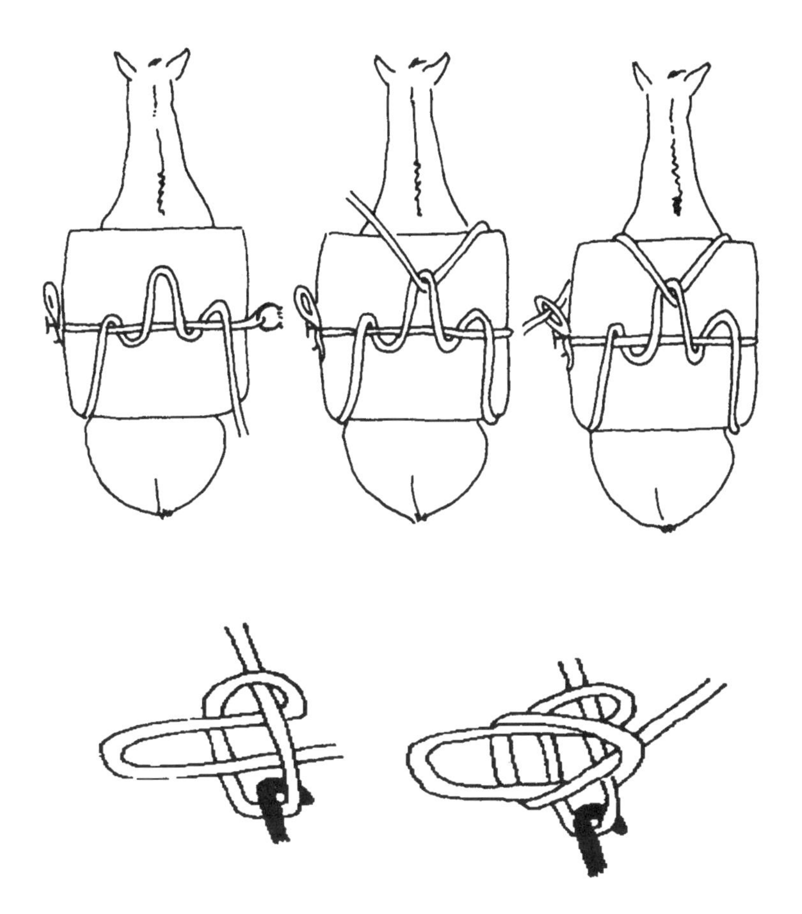

This hitch is to be started about two-thirds back on the pack, because all the pull is toward the front of the pack when tightening.

Start with a loop over the hook on the lash cinch, tie a slip knot and put a half-hitch over it to keep it from slipping. The loop should point forward. The lash cinch hook points to the rear. Use the squaw hitch if you are short on rope or if you have a tall pack. Caution: Do not draw the gooseneck so far forward that the rope rubs the horse's withers.

Double Diamond

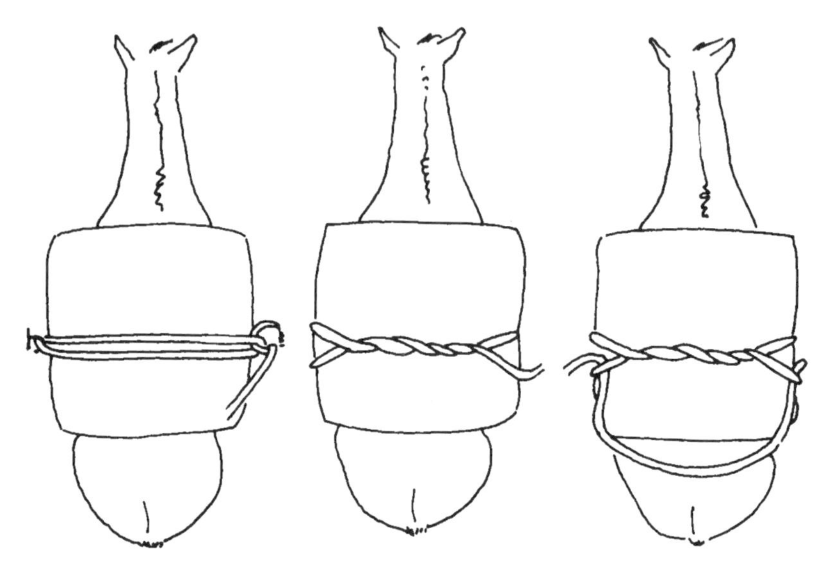

Use the double diamond on large, tall packs; it takes a lot of rope (45') but holds a pack very well. Take the rope over and through the back side of the cinch ring on the off side. To make the diamond on each side, always take the right rope over the left two to three times on each side

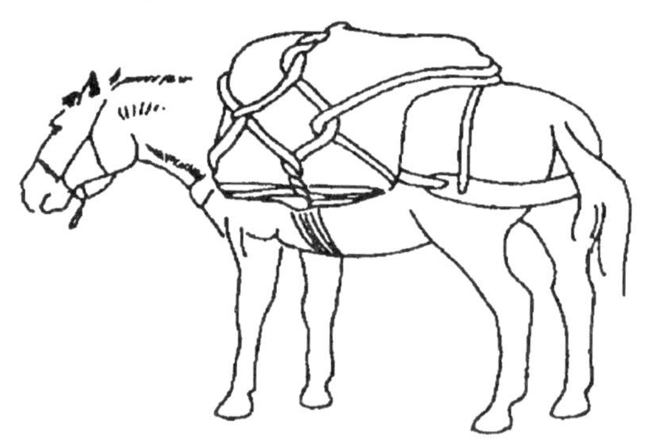

to assure the twist on top will hold. If the right rope is used on one side and the left on the other side, the twist on top will come undone. A stick of 6" or so put between the ropes on top will act as a safety to keep the ropes from coming untwisted if you are not sure you have the hitch tied correctly. But that makes an ugly hitch. **We don't like "ugly hitches."**

Arizona or Basket Hitch

A one-person hitch

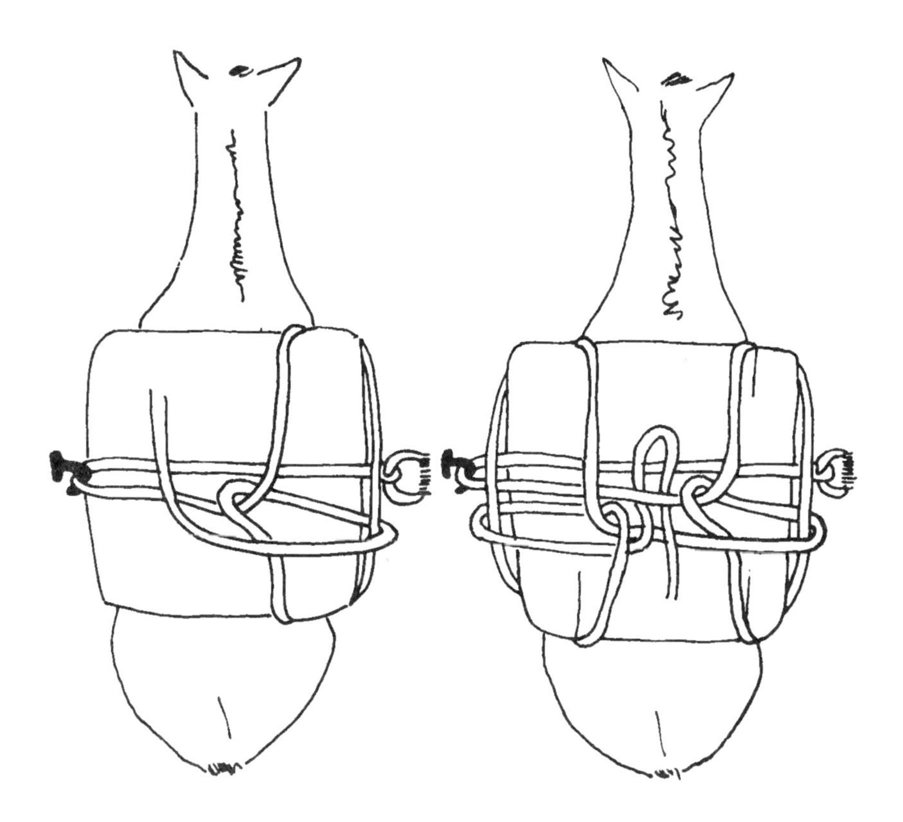

This is an excellent hitch to hold the panniers out and away from the animal's side and shoulder, so rubbing does not occur. To do this, pull down on the lash rope (after the loop around each pannier is made), then pull the rope up, which will pull the panniers out and hold them out. At least 45' of rope is needed to do this one-person hitch.

Basket Sling

This sling works well for bales of hay, sacks of grain and quarters of meat or any mantied load.

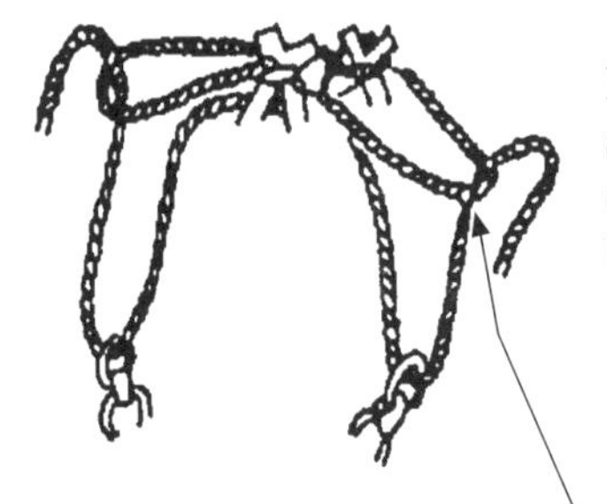

Divide a 30' to 40' rope in two equal parts so that about 20' is on each side of the saddle. Use a clove hitch on the front cross-buck or tie to the front arches of a decker.

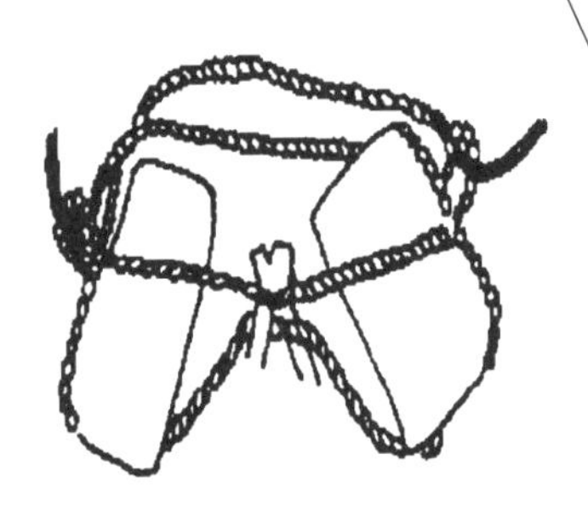

Tie a slip knot here and half hitch it so it won't slip. Then throw the running end over the top of the bales and tie to the loop on the opposite side.

After securing the bales with the basket sling, a manta can be thrown over the load and then a double diamond hitch over that. Take a look from the rear to be sure the load is balanced before you tighten and tie off.

Barrel Sling

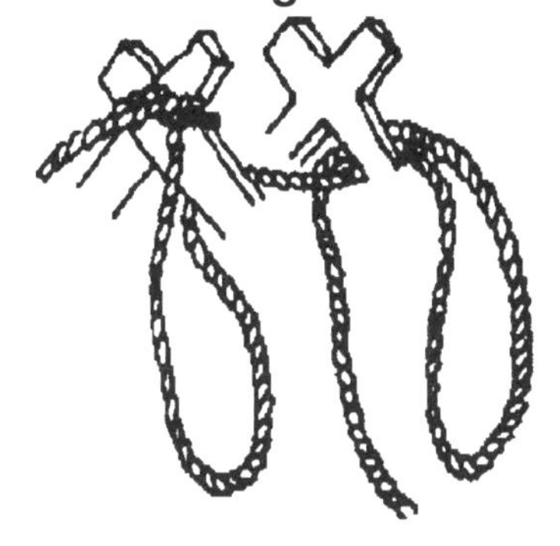

Balance from front to rear is the critical aspect of this hitch. Get a good bight on each end to secure barrel or bale. Then throw a diamond or double diamond over the whole load.

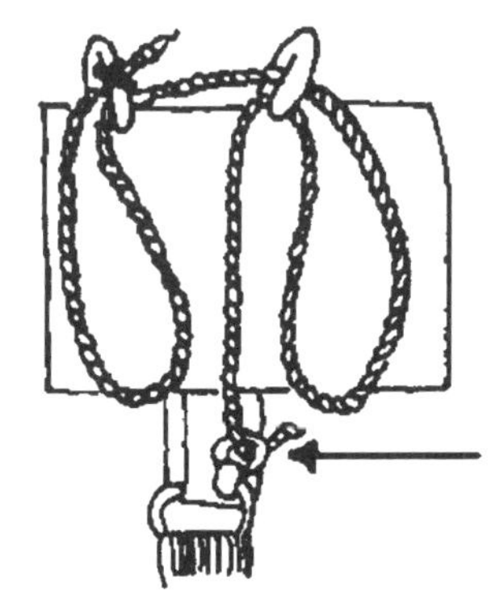

An extra ring works well and saves pulling the horse's hair around the cinch ring.

Be proud of your pack, and don't tie any "ugly diamonds."

Tying Off a Hitch

An easy, quick release slip knot is handy in case of a wreck, when you may need to release a pack or an animal in a hurry.

Tie back to the **lash cinch ring** or to a **solid corner** above a place where two ropes cross and where the knot will not slip and loosen the entire pack.

Be sure all slack is taken out of the lash rope on both sides of the pack. Work the rope back from scratch, feeding the slack to your partner as he or she keeps it tight and ties it off.

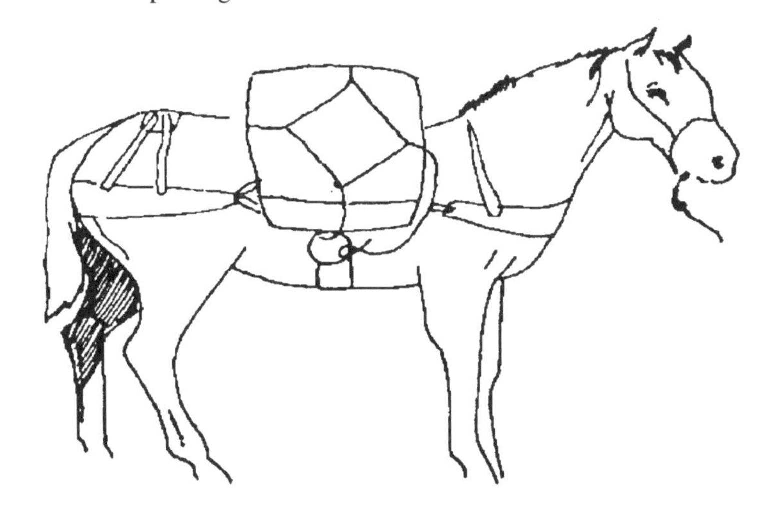

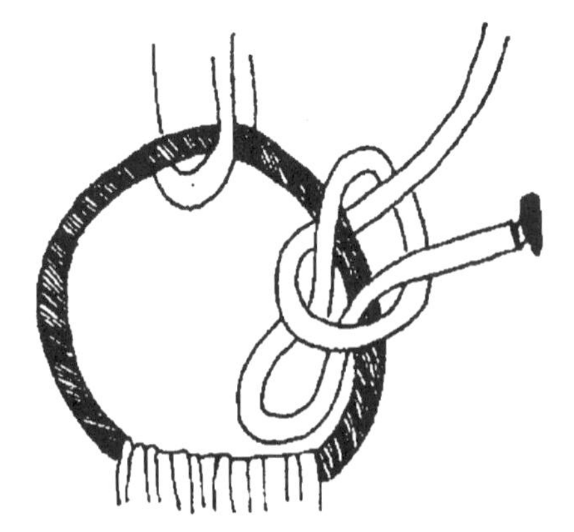

After hitch is tied off, be sure to tuck in the loose end so it does not drag in the mud or catch on a rock or tree, or . . . **WHOA!** another wreck.

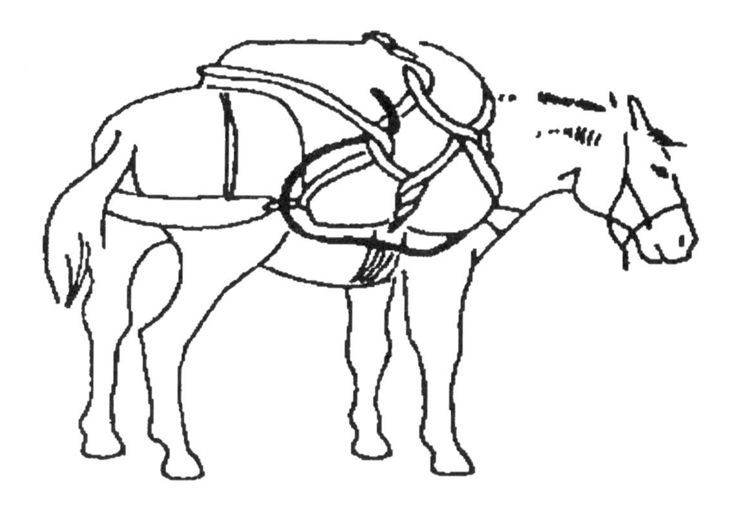

Tying off to a solid corner. If extra rope is leftover, chain it through the slip knot loop and tuck it under the back side of the pack.

Throw a half hitch over the slip knot loop to keep it from coming loose.

Get it Tight Partner

Get it tight, or you'll have to stop on the trail . . . in a rainstorm or blizzard . . . on the edge of a cliff . . . in the middle of a rock slide . . . or somewhere tougher than where you started. If a hitch is done properly, tightened and tied, it should last for the day without being retied or adjusted. Some pack animals "swell up" more than others when saddled, and some packs will settle more than others, so this is variable. It helps if you feed out the slack in the lash rope and get it tight the first time.

Before the panniers go on, be sure the pack saddle cinches are tight. Then load up.

Here's a typical way of arranging a pack:

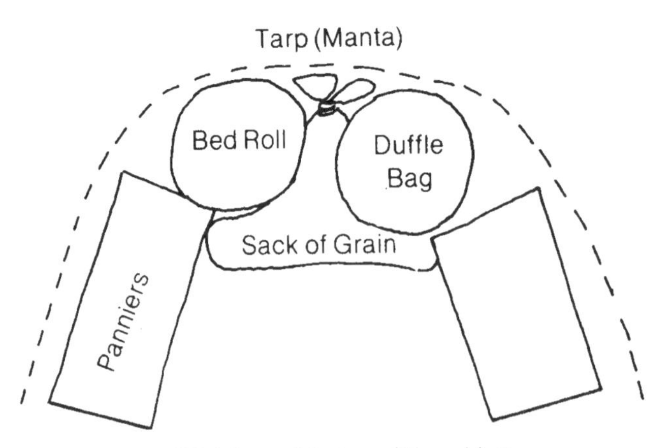

Weight and balance is crucial!

Tying on a Sheepherder Stove and a Bucket

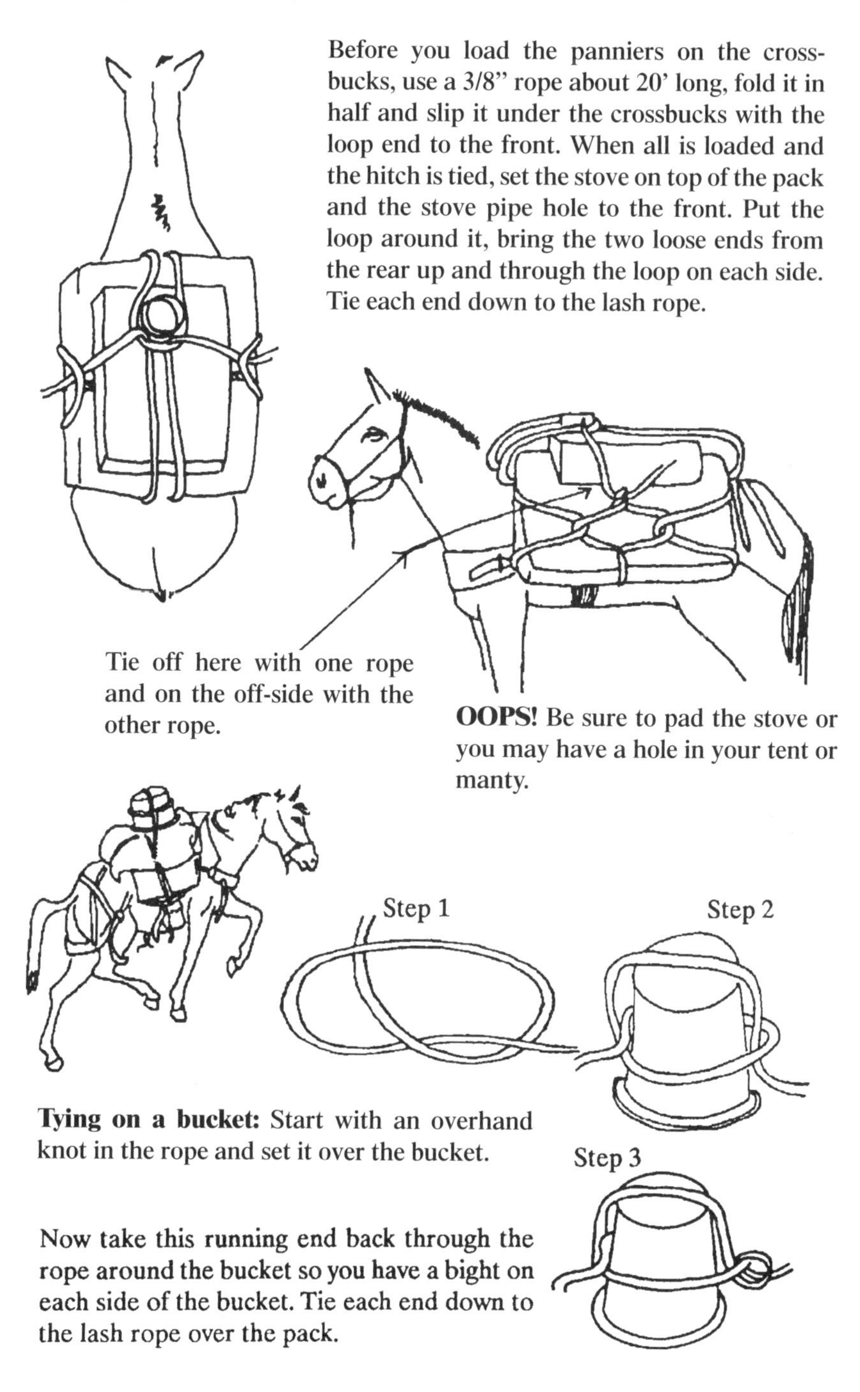

Before you load the panniers on the cross-bucks, use a 3/8" rope about 20' long, fold it in half and slip it under the crossbucks with the loop end to the front. When all is loaded and the hitch is tied, set the stove on top of the pack and the stove pipe hole to the front. Put the loop around it, bring the two loose ends from the rear up and through the loop on each side. Tie each end down to the lash rope.

Tie off here with one rope and on the off-side with the other rope.

OOPS! Be sure to pad the stove or you may have a hole in your tent or manty.

Tying on a bucket: Start with an overhand knot in the rope and set it over the bucket.

Now take this running end back through the rope around the bucket so you have a bight on each side of the bucket. Tie each end down to the lash rope over the pack.

Packing Meat

Use the basket sling on a pack saddle or on a stock saddle for packing meat. To help maintain balance when packing half an elk, moose or deer on a stock saddle, after load is balanced, cut a hole in the hide and slip it over the saddle horn. Then complete the sling and tie it off. This is just one way of rigging a sling to pack meat. Other methods work well also. If you want added security, cover meat with a manta and tie a double diamond over the entire pack.

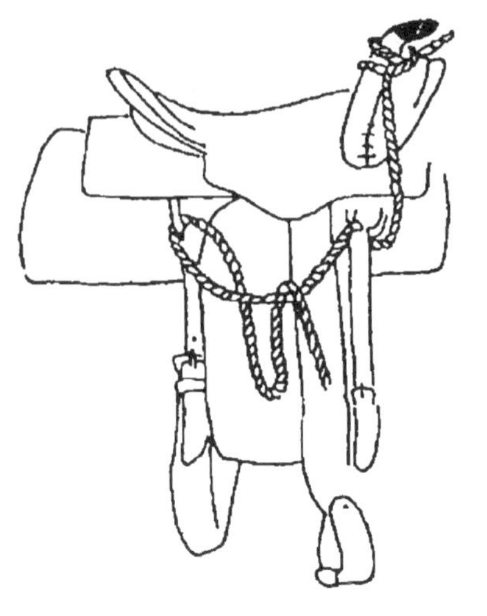

The basket sling on a stock saddle works well for packing meat as author and son demonstrate.

CHAPTER 4

Knots

- General Purpose Knots
  - Raid
  - Clove Hitch
  - Honda
  - Bowline
  - Slip or Manger Knot
  - Figure 8
  - Overhand
  - Sheep Shank
  - Square Knot
- Knots for Halter Ring or Lash Cinch
  - Anchor Bend
  - Non-Slipping Halter Tie
- Knots for Tying a Pack String Together
  - Pigtail Knot
  - Tail Knot
- Rope End Knots
  - Wall Knot
  - Crown Knot
  - Single Mathew Walker
- Emergency Rope Halter
- Rope Splices
  - Crown Splice
  - Eye Splice
  - Carrick Bend
  - Short Splice

GENERAL PURPOSE KNOTS

Raid

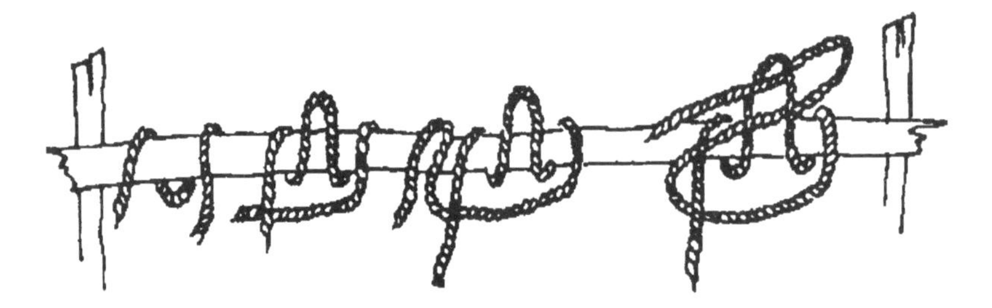

This is the old bank robbers' "get-away-fast" knot. Try it!

Clove Hitch (two half hitches)

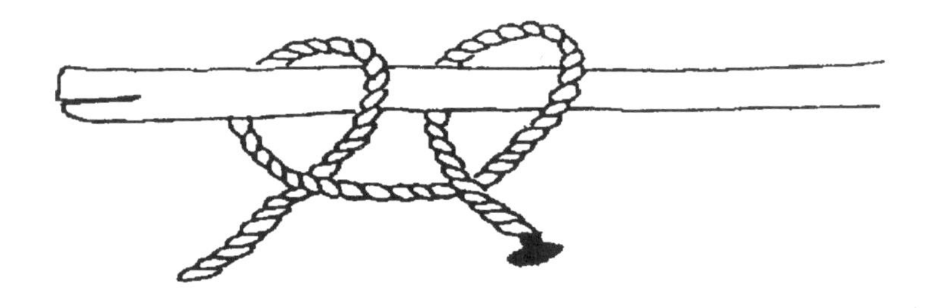

Honda (must have the end knot to prevent from slipping through)

Bowline

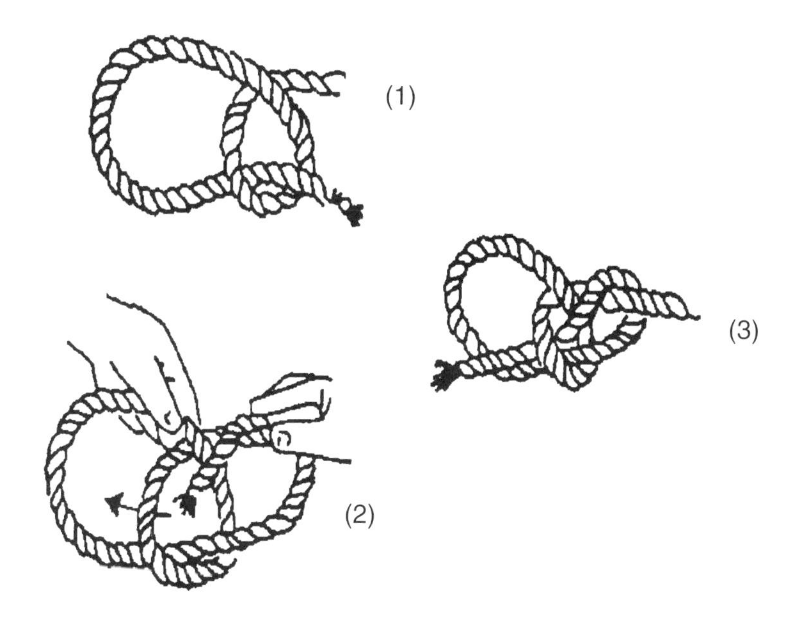

Slip or Manger Knot (left-handed)

Can be tied by passing rope under or over tie rail.

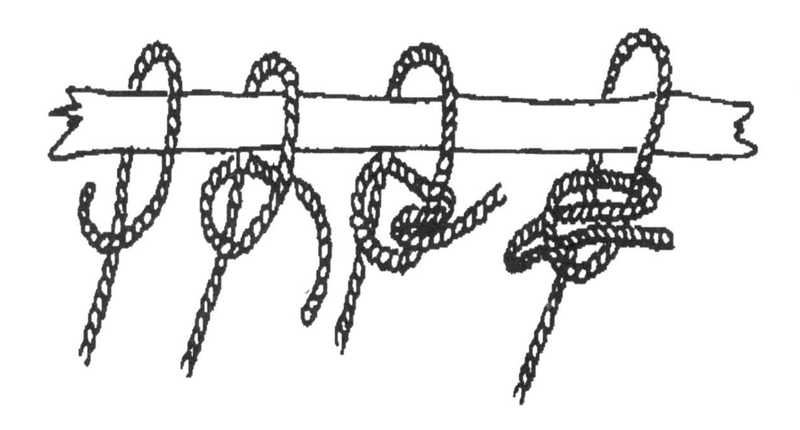

Figure 8

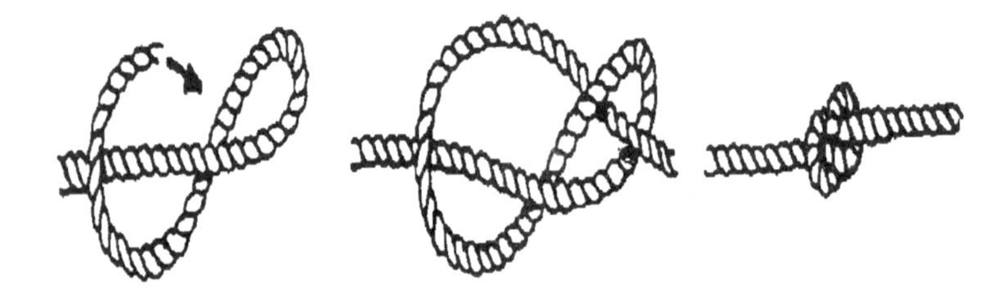

This knot is much easier to untie than the overhand knot. It is larger, stronger and does not injure rope fibers. It is the best knot to use to keep the end of a rope from running out of a tackle or pulley.

To tie: Make an underhand loop. Bring end around and over the standing part. Pass the end under and then up through the loop. Draw up tight.

Overhand

This is the simplest and smallest of all knots. In general, use it only on small cord and twine, because it jams, is hard to untie and often injures the fiber.

To tie: Make a loop near the end of the rope and pass the end under and up through the loop. Draw up tight.

Sheepshank

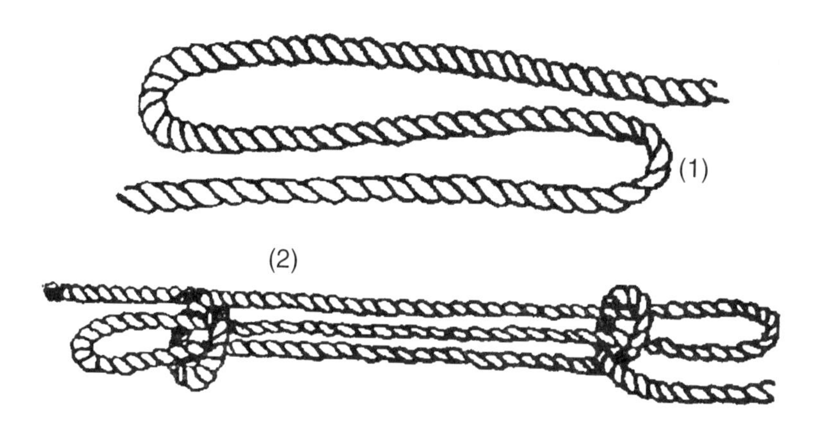

The sheepshank is used to shorten a rope.

To tie: Form an “S” loop as shown in the top diagram. Then with one free end, make a half hitch and slip it over one of the loops. Tighten; repeat procedure with the other loop.

Square Knot

The square knot is used to tie two ropes together and is referred to as the universal package knot.

To tie: Pass the left end over and under the right end. Curve what is now the left end towards the right. Cross what is now the right end over and under the left end. Draw up tight.

Don’t tie the weak granny knot. Remember that the square knot presents two ends lying under one loop and over the opposite loop — while the granny presents one end under and one over on both loops.

KNOTS USED TO TIE TO A HALTER RING OR TO A LASH CINCH

Anchor Bend

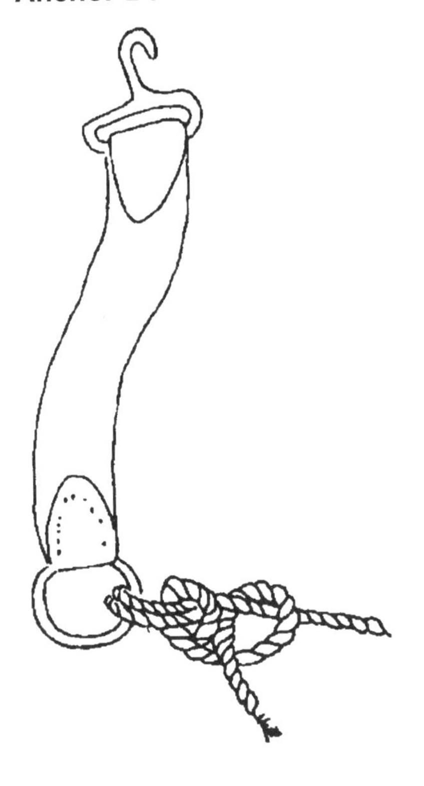

The anchor bend is used to secure a rope to a ring.

To tie: Give the rope two turns about the ring, creating a larger wear surface than with the common hitches. Finish the knot by making two overhand knots to the standing end of the rope.

Non-Slipping Halter Tie

Use the non-slipping halter tie to fasten a halter rope to a ring.

To tie: Place the end of the rope through the ring and around beneath the long portion of the rope. Move the end of the rope as indicated by arrow. Draw up tightly.

KNOTS FOR TYING A STRING OF PACK ANIMALS TOGETHER

Pigtail Knot Use small breakable baling twine or 1/4" hemp or cotton and tie to sawbuck. Leave loop in the end to tie to the lead rope.

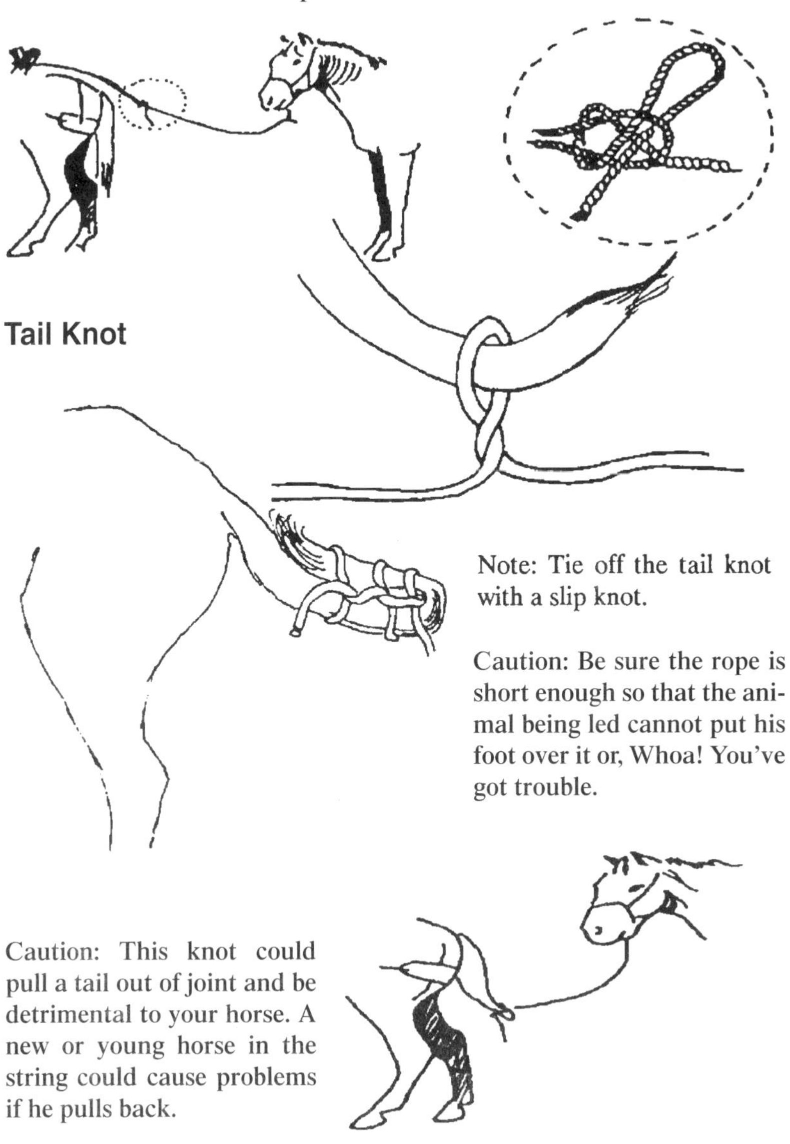

Tail Knot

Note: Tie off the tail knot with a slip knot.

Caution: Be sure the rope is short enough so that the animal being led cannot put his foot over it or, Whoa! You've got trouble.

Caution: This knot could pull a tail out of joint and be detrimental to your horse. A new or young horse in the string could cause problems if he pulls back.

ROPE END KNOTS

Wall Knot

Among the rope end fastenings that are easily and quickly made, the wall

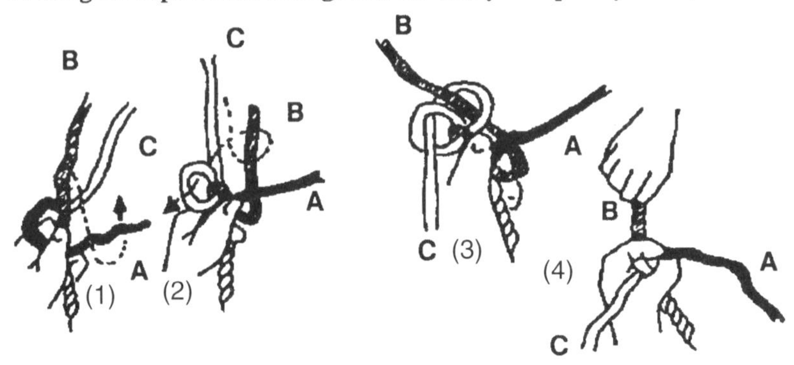

knot is the most used. To tie: For a small rope, unlay the strands about 3". Hold the rope in the left hand, loose strands upward. With the right hand grasp the end of strand A and bring it across the rope, forming a loop and allowing the end to hang free. Hold the loose end in position with the left thumb. Grasp strand B, pass it under strand A (see arrow in figure above) and hold it against the rope with the thumb of the left hand. Again, with the right hand, grasp strand C, pass it under B and up through the first loop formed, as indicated by the arrow and shown in the middle illustrations. Draw each strand gradually until the knot is tight.

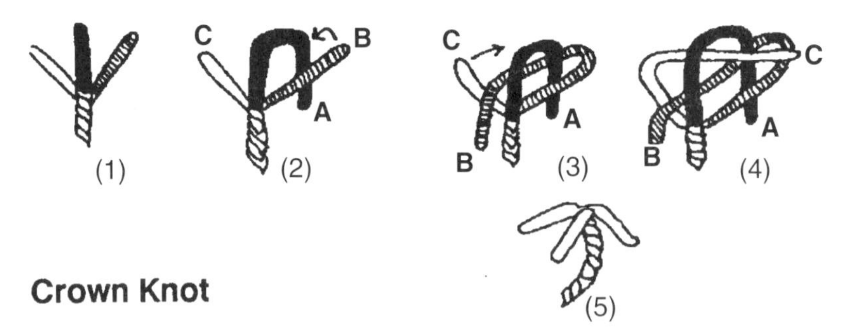

Crown Knot

Loop strand A between strands B and C as shown above. Bring strand B around the loop formed by strand A. Pass strand C over strand B and through the loop formed by strand A. Tighten ends to form the crown knot.

Single Mathew Walker

The single Mathew Walker is one of the most permanent of the end knots and one of the most difficult. The easiest way to tie it is to construct a wall knot, then continue as follows.

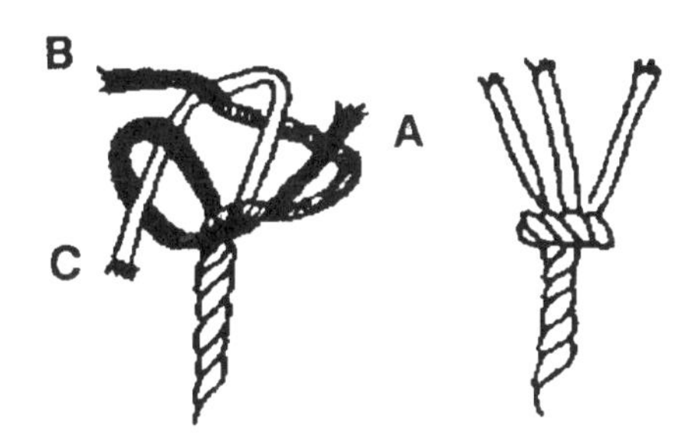

To tie: Pass end A through the loop with B, bend B through the loop with C and C through loop A. Tighten the knot gradually by drawing each of the ends.

Emergercy Rope Halter

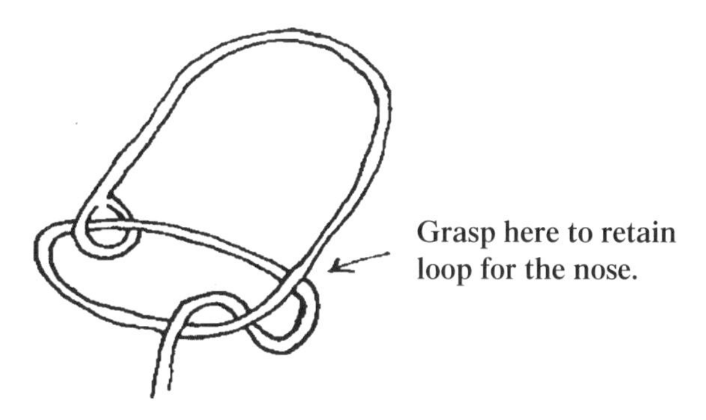

ROPE SPLICES

Crown Splice

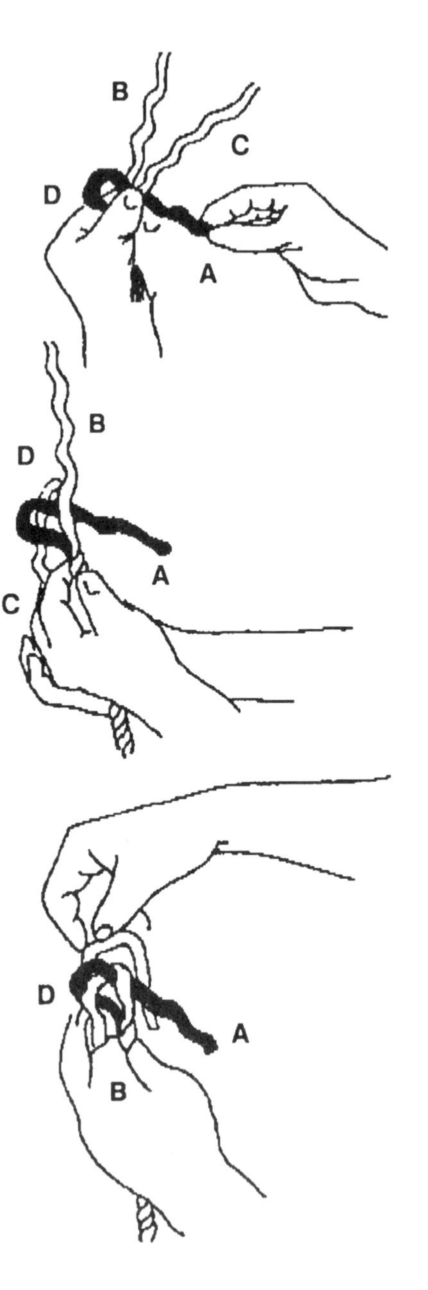

To start the crown splice, hold the rope in your left hand. With the right hand, unlay the rope about 6" from the end. Then place or lay the strand A to your left between the other two strands B and C to form a loop D.

Split each strand in half and cut off. Use the remaining half to braid back in. This will make the splice smaller and more the size of the original rope.

In the next step, lay the strand C to your right between the loop D and the middle strand B.

Next, bring the end of the center strand B through the loop D from the rear in the direction toward you.

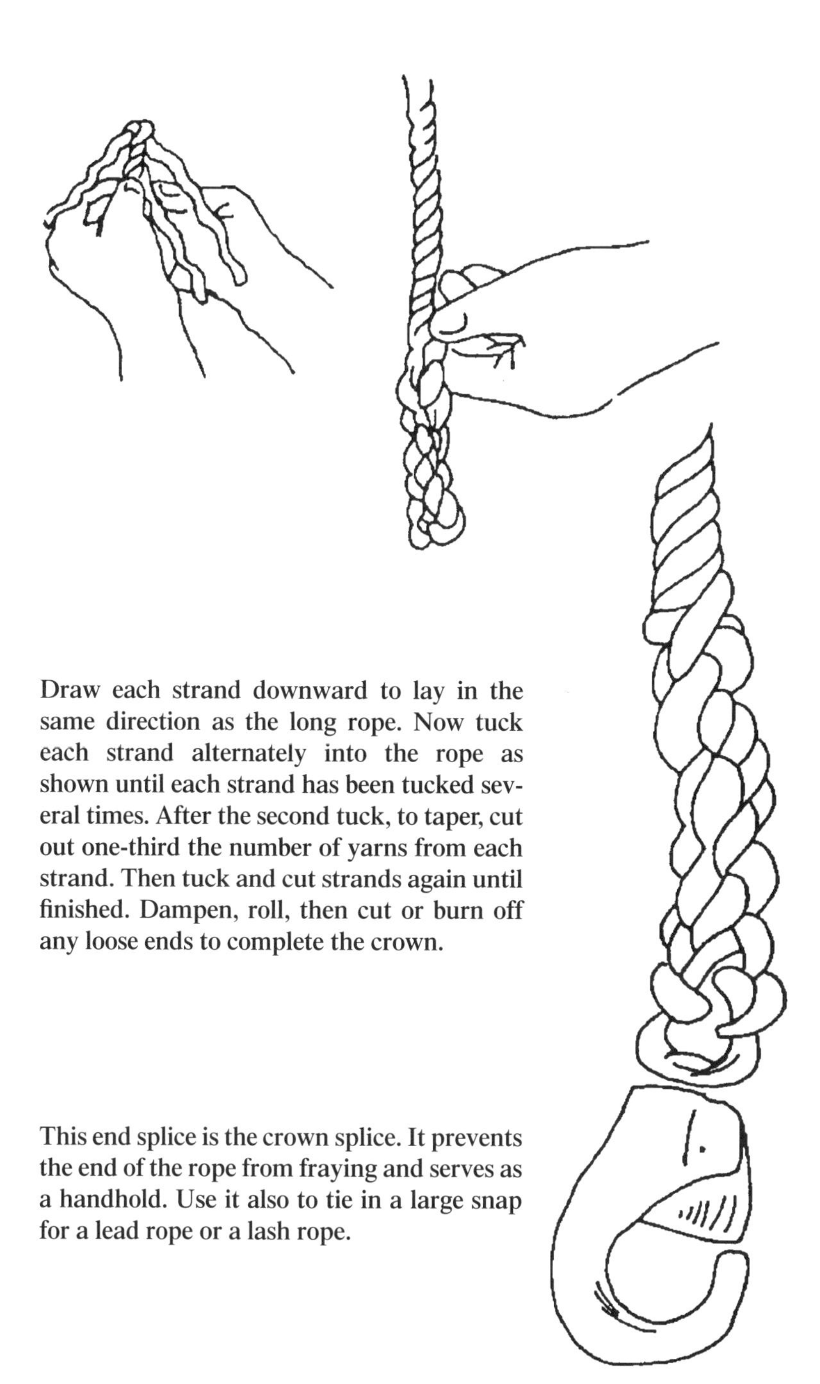

Draw each strand downward to lay in the same direction as the long rope. Now tuck each strand alternately into the rope as shown until each strand has been tucked several times. After the second tuck, to taper, cut out one-third the number of yarns from each strand. Then tuck and cut strands again until finished. Dampen, roll, then cut or burn off any loose ends to complete the crown.

This end splice is the crown splice. It prevents the end of the rope from fraying and serves as a handhold. Use it also to tie in a large snap for a lead rope or a lash rope.

Eye Splice

The eye splice is used in making halters, in the end of a rope for mooring and in place of the honda knot for making a lariat. The end, after being unlaid, is bent around to form the eye and is spliced into its own strands of the standing part.

Carrick Bend

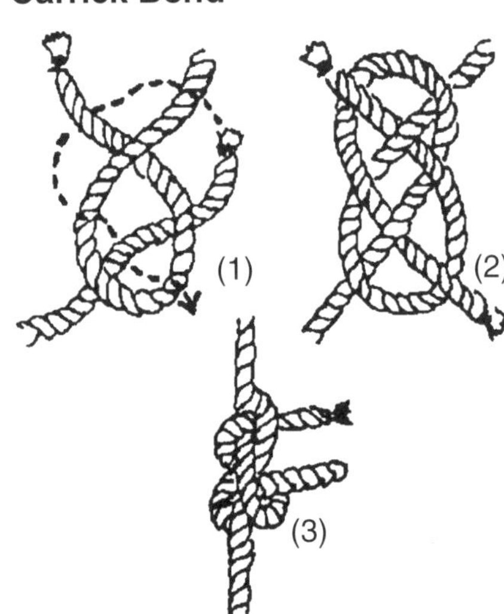

The carrick bend is a strong knot that cannot jam and unties easily. Under strain it always draws up tight and correctly.

To tie: With one rope end form an underhand loop. With both the free end and standing part pointing away from you, start the second rope end beneath both sides of the loop. Cross it over the standing part of the first rope, then under the free end of the first rope, then over the left side of the loop. Cross it under itself, and let the second free end lie over the right side of the loop. Finish by pulling ends so knot is tightened.

Short Splice

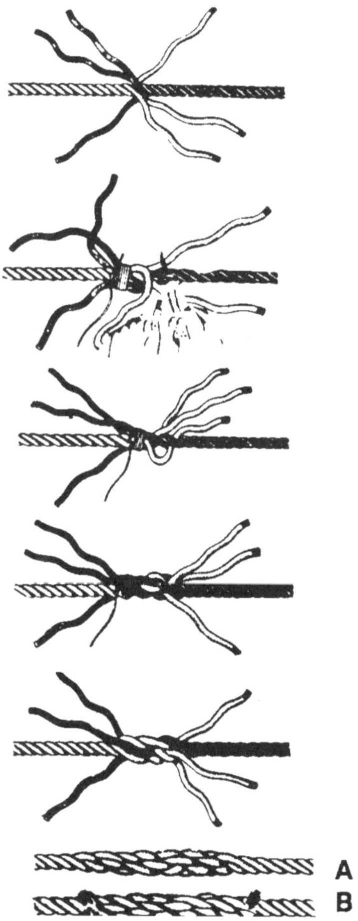

The short splice is used to join two ropes together or two ends of the same rope to make a "sling" or continuous wreath or rope. A sling is tied around an object to attach it to a hook for hoisting. The short splice, though the strongest of the splices, cannot be used on a rope that is to run through a correctly sized pulley.

How to tie splice: Unlay the strands of the ropes for a short distance, whip ends of the strands to prevent untwisting and put together as in diagram at right, alternating the strands from each end. Now tie down one set of strands temporarily. Taking any strand of the opposite set, tuck it over and under one strand of the rope. Tuck against the twist or "lay" of the rope. The tuck goes over one strand, under the second and out between the second and third.

Repeat the same procedure with the other two strands from the same end of the rope.

A

B

Remove tie from other strands. Repeat operation on the other side of the rope. Continue two more tucks for each of the six strands.

To finish, roll and pound rope on hard surface. (Leave ends of strands as shown in sketch B.) Don't cut ends of strands off too close!

For the tapered splice (see sketch A), which gives better service, take two more tucks with each strand, but before the first tuck, cut out one-third the number of yarns from each strand. Tuck, then cut strands again, removing one-half of the remaining yarns and tuck once again.

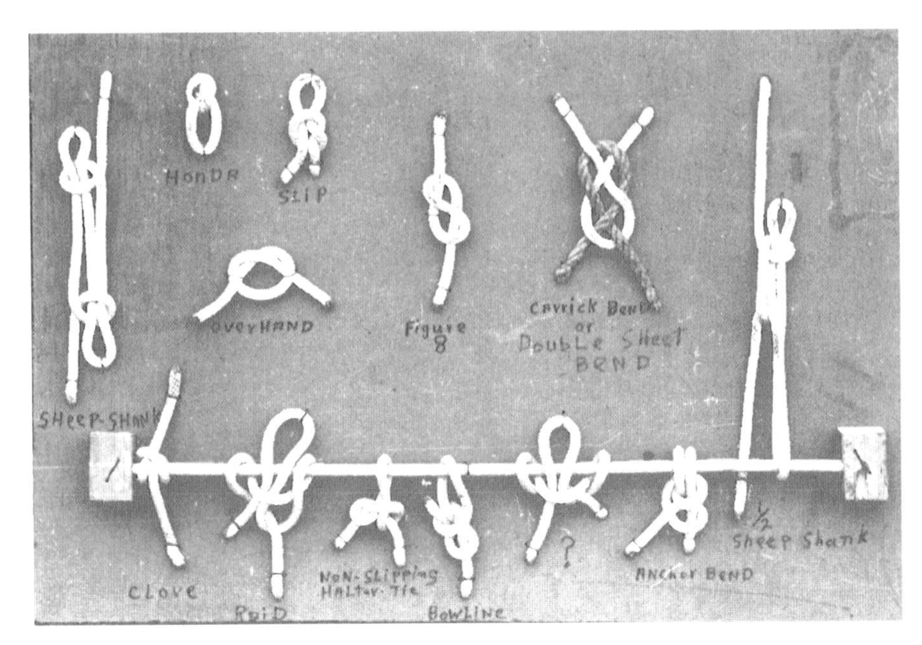

Did you learn and remember all the knots? This rope board may help you remember and practice them.

CHAPTER 5

Planning Your Pack Trip

FACTORS TO CONSIDER

1. What is the purpose of the trip? Sightseeing, hunting, fishing, tour of range and forest?

2. What is the destination of the trip? Will a loop trip be made? Will it be an "up and back?" Will it be a "go on through" situation?

3. Will you end up at the same location as you started, or will someone need to move the vehicles to meet you?

4. How far must the animals be trailered to the jump-off point?

5. How rough is the country? Are there dangerous places where people should dismount and lead their horses across slides or drop-offs? Are there shelf trails or is the country gentle and rolling?

6. How far can you travel in a day?
    - Depends on those participating: age, physical condition, trip purpose.
    - Depends on conditioning of horses.
    - Seven to ten miles per day can be covered if horses and people are in good physical shape and if the country is not too rough.
    - More than 20 miles per day can be grueling for man and beast.

7. How often to move camp?
    - How long will you be gone?
    - How much country will be covered?
    - Can you ride from a base camp in three or four directions without moving camp?
    - Can smaller spike camps be set up?

8. Are permits required for recreational use for campsites and other situations.?
    - Check with the USDA Forest Service, Bureau of Land Management, National Park Service or any other agencies controlling your destination area.

9. Are you going into bear country?
    - If so what are the requirements for food, fires, trash, etc?

USE COMMON SENSE!

Don't take unnecessary chances. Be prepared. Be in good condition. Play it safe. Plan ahead. Be comfortable. Don't put too much stress on people or animals.

SAMPLE TRIP ITINERARY

Plan ahead. Do it right and have a good trip!

6:00 a.m.	Guide and wrangler: Catch horses, feed and water them.
7:00	Everyone out of bed.
7:30	Breakfast served.
8:00	Load horses and truck them about three miles to trail head.
8:30	Saddle horses. Pack and arrange gear. Match up horses, riders and saddles. (Use scale to weigh panniers.)
10:00	Leave for 7-mile fishing trip.
11:00	Ten-minute rest break if needed. Check packs, cinches and riders.
12:30 p.m.	Thirty-minute lunch break: Lunches in saddle bags.
3:00	Arrive at lake. Unload pack horses, then unsaddle all horses. Stake them on hilltop behind camp (where camp is between horses and exit from lake). Tie at least three horses; hobble the others.
4:00	Set up tents and camp.
4:15	Gather firewood or pack it in if above timberline.
4:30	Distribute gear; inflate air mattresses; fish if you like.
5:30	Begin meal preparations, and organize camp kitchen.
6:30	Prepare and serve dinner.
7:30	Wash dishes and make preparations for breakfast. Water and feed horses. Catch loose horses and tie them for the night.
8:30	Make and enjoy campfire before hitting the sack.

Second Day

6:30 a.m.	Rise and shine.
7:00	Feed and water horses. Turn half of them loose with hobbles to graze.
7:30	Prepare and serve breakfast.
8:30	Fish, hike or sightsee.
11:30 - noon	Prepare and serve lunch.
1:00 p.m.	Wash dishes and thaw steaks for evening.
1:30	Let other horses graze; tie up first half (use grain to catch). Rest, fish or hike.
5:30 - 6:30	Prepare and serve dinner.
7:30	Wash dishes and prepare for moving camp.
8:30 - 10:00	Campfire and popcorn party. Water and feed horses. Tie horses up for the night. Problem horses should be hobbled and tied. It takes the fun out of a trip to have to chase horses in the middle of the night.

THE CAMP

Camping in the great outdoors can be a pleasant and memorable experience, especially on a pack trip where one gets away from phone, people, pollution and everyday problems. It can also be unpleasant if the camp itself is not a good one.

The Essentials for a Comfortable Camp: Find grass for your stock, water for man and beast and shelter of some trees to break the wind and provide firewood too.

Tents: First of all, your "home away from home" needs to be suitable, waterproof and in good condition. You need to be able to stand up in a

Gary Keimig of Dubois, Wyoming, in his painting, "Dunoir Wilderness Camp," shows many features of a high mountain camp.

tent, have a comfortable bed and an area to store your gear with a little extra elbow room. This is especially true if bad weather sets in and people are confined to a tent. When rainy or snowy weather sets in, you are always glad you took the time back home to weatherproof your tent. It can rain or snow on short notice in the high country. Don't put your tent in a hollow, because cold air settles in low spots or you can get flooded out.

Don't overcrowd your tents. Three to four people in a 10' x 12' wall tent is comfortable. More than four, with gear, is a crowd.

Campsite: The camp location is important to your comfort on a pack trip. Don't pitch your tents in a low, wet, boggy area or put them near old dead trees that could blow over and smash your outfit. Find a good, level spot or you will roll or slide downhill in your sleeping bag all night.

Follow the USDA Forest Service's 200-foot rule. Keep your camp and all stock 200' from lakes, streams, meadows, trails and neighboring campers.

If you prefer morning sun or evening sun, set your camp accordingly if you have a choice. Some sun is really nice as it provides warmth.

Water and Wood: Both are important for people and horses, so camp near a creek. A spring is even better. Scout upstream for pollution or a dead animal in the stream before using creek water. Caution should be used in drinking raw stream water. Be prepared to boil, filter and or chemically treat your drinking water to insure your health. This is a must to keep everyone healthy and having fun. It is nice to have firewood around, but in many places above timberline, you may have to pack in your wood.

Storage: Have a separate cook tent in which to store supplies. A smaller canvas lean-to or shelter works well for storing other equipment.

Store saddles, pads and panniers up off the ground where they can air and dry out. Cover them at night to protect from the frost and dew. This is a good place to use those mantas!

The Outdoor Privy: This is a necessity. Dig a hole at least 200' away from camp, water and trails, and fasten a tarp to the trees to provide privacy. Tie the paper to a tree with some baling wire or place it on a stick. To keep the toilet paper dry, cover the roll with a plastic bag. Cover the hole well when breaking camp.

Trash: Pack your trash to take out with you. Be sure all cans and rubbish are put in a garbage bag. Smash cans flat to save space. Keep the high country beautiful. Pack out some of the other guy's junk, too. Cans are noisy, so pack with paper if you have a "spook" for a pack horse. If you "pack it in, pack it out" along with any other trash you may find.

Campfire: Be sure your campfire is out cold. Pour water over it, and cover it with dirt. Always pack a shovel and a canvas bucket. Return the area to its natural state. "Leave no trace" is an important philosophy so everyone can enjoy the beauty of our public lands.

Horses: If you want a good night's sleep, keep the horses tied, staked or hobbled away from the tents. Otherwise they'll be tangled in the tent ropes, into the grain or just "moseying" by all night. It is reassuring, however, to hear the ting-a-ling of that good ole bell (that you nearly forgot) and to know that the critters that brought you and will take you out, are still in camp. **Going footback** is fine with some folks, but horseback sure saves lots of steps. Always water your horses downstream. Rotate their grazing areas so they don't trample or over graze the meadow. Be sure to scatter "horse apples" when breaking camp.

STAKING A HORSE

Staking is a handy thing to teach your horse, especially if he participates with you in trail rides and camping trips.

If you plan to stake your horse, it is wise to give him some lessons at home before going to the mountains. And when you actually do stake him those first few times, you'll want to be nearby to get him out of a bad tangle if he gets caught in the rope. Most horses learn fast. After they have gotten their feet in the rope several times, they watch where they put their feet and graze systematically in a circle to avoid getting tangled up in the rope.

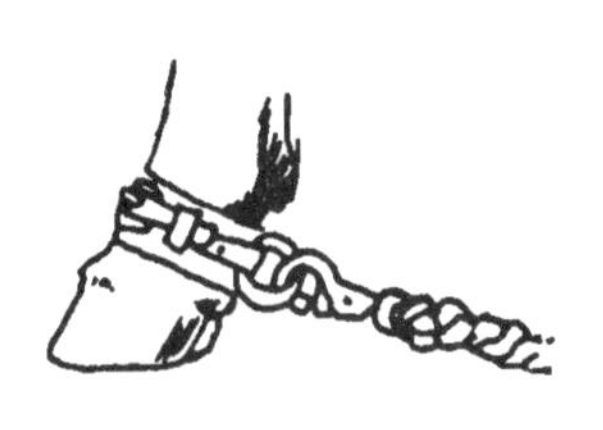

After your horse has learned to stake, it's best to stake him by a front foot. He won't get tangled up so easily and he'll have a lot less trouble. But you want to start him out tied by the halter. It is easier for him to learn what it's all about if he is already halter broken and doesn't fight this restraint.

Some horses are spooky about ropes, but there are ways you can get around a rope-shy horse's fears before you ever stake him. A few **sacking-out** lessons with a rope can help. By rubbing the rope over his body and letting it move about his legs, he'll soon realize that the rope isn't going to hurt him.

With some horses it helps to let them graze a few times in a small enclosure just **dragging a rope** so they can get accustomed to having a rope around their feet and learn not to step on it. The horse learns that when he steps on the rope and it holds his head down, there's no real cause for alarm or excitement (some horses seem to get claustrophobia at having their heads held low), and that by picking up the proper foot his head will be free again.

It's not impossible to start a horse out staked by a front foot instead of by the halter. You might want to try this method if your horse is spooky about having his head caught low. But if you do it this way, prepare the horse by letting him adjust gradually to having a foot tied to something. A few short lessons with hobbles will help the horse get used to having his front feet restrained. After he is used to the hobbles, put him in a corral with a short length of rope fastened to one front pastern. As he moves around, he learns not to be upset or frightened or to resist when he steps on the rope and it inhibits his front leg. He soon learns to maneuver his feet accordingly.

When you actually stake the horse, you'll need a large, soft cotton rope at least an inch in diameter. This won't burn him as badly as a small rope or a hard-twist one if he gets wound up and fights it. A stake rope should have **two swivels** in it, one on each end, to keep it from twisting as the horse moves around.

The first few times you stake your horse, do it in a **flat, grassy place** that has no rocks or sharp objects to hurt him if he gets tangled as he grazes or if he throws himself. It might also be a good idea to keep him hungry for a few hours before his first staking. Then he will be too busy grazing to make any real attempt at getting loose.

When staking a horse, use something around his pastern that won't cut or cause a rope burn. A leather strap with some kind of padding on the inside works well, and you can put a ring around the strap or through the buckle with which to fasten the rope. **Sheepskin lining** attached inside works well for padding.

A shod horse can get his hind shoe caught in the halter if he happens to try to scratch his ear with a hind foot. Staking by a halter is also just generally inconvenient for the horse, as he is almost sure to step on the rope with a front foot or get the rope around a hind foot. Sometimes he can get into a mess that's hard to get out of if his head is restrained by the halter and stake rope.

Staked by a front foot, the horse isn't as likely to get entangled, because the rope stays on the ground as he grazes and moves about. He isn't as apt to get his hind legs caught in it as he turns. With the rope tied to his halter, it comes off the ground each time the horse raises his head, moving high up on his legs as he moves and turns. Staking by a front foot saves a lot of trouble.

After your horse has learned to stake, you will find camping and traveling with him a lot easier and less complicated. You won't have the worry of a place to keep him or the problem of taking along a lot of feed. All you'll need is adequate rope and foot strap, a stake and a grassy place. Your horse will appreciate the chance to fill his belly instead of being tied up all night. A stake is not always necessary but is handy if there are no trees or rocks around to tie up to.

Staking out by a foot or by the halter could be dangerous if a horse is badly spooked. This could result in a broken neck, dislocated shoulder or other injuries. This is a consideration if you have a valuable horse, or for that matter any horse not well trained to staking.

Staking out: Horses away from the campsite are tied head to tail in pairs. They won't go far!

For overnight, tie up with a slip knot. In case of emergency you can pull it out. Use hobbles in addition for those tough, smart critters to keep them home at night.

CHAPTER 6

Pre-Trip Training and Conditioning

Training at Home

Be sure you have trained and practicied at home everything you plan to do with your horse.

1. Staking and hobbling.
2. Loading and unloading panniers.
3. Pulling the lash rope around the pack.
4. Saddle and unsaddle to get pack horse used to the breeching and breast collar.

The more you can do at home, the more enjoyable and trouble free your trip will be for you and your animals. Anything you plan to do on your trip, you should practice and do at home first.

Pre-Trip Conditioning

Generally speaking many of the people who plan to take a pack trip are not in top notch shape and neither are many of their animals. Getting in shape to face higher altitudes, steep terrain and perhaps inclement weather, is a must. Riding two to five miles, two to three times a week prior to your trip will help you and your animals.

1. Muscles will be firmed up.
2. Back and cinch areas will be toughened up.
3. Lung capacity will be increased.
4. Excess weight will be reduced.
5. Perspiration will be minimized.

Make sure you, your guests and your animals are in good physical shape before you go. The high country brings on extra stressful situations, and you must be prepared to expend the extra energy to meet the demands of Mother Nature.

The Spirit of Packing

Artist Dave Mathis from Reno, Nevada, captures the spirit of packing.

1. Clean, cool, refreshing air.
2. Beautiful mountain scenery.
3. Solitude.
4. No phones, vehicles, noise and smog.
5. Elbow room to relax.

With all this wonderful experience also comes the responsiblity to care for and protect our public lands for future generations.

CHAPTER 7

Persuasion and Restraint

PERSUASION AND RESTRAINT

A FEW THOUGHTS ABOUT HANDLING HORSES

Which will it be? Can you persuade your animal to cooperate or will restraint need to be used? Every horse, mule or burro is as different as every human handler. Every person and every critter has its own hang-ups, fears, problems and disposition.

Mother Nature created the horse with several natural instincts: **self protection** and **flight** are two that affect handlers. The horse is basically timid and easily frightened. He frequently acts to save himself from real or imagined dangers. When a horse is restrained his strong instinct for flight is affected, and he may panic. At this point he may hurt himself or the handler. Another example might be when a twitch or war bridle is applied. The horse may strike out at the danger. Kicking may be the result of the fear of ropes over the hocks and hindquarters.

Restraints are normally applied in an attempt to inhibit natural instints such as running away, shying, kicking, striking and bucking. In applying these restraints, the handler must use some horse psychology and a lot of horse sense. **The goal of any handler has to be to instill confidence and trust in the horse to create the desired behavior.**

DISPOSITION

How to recognize and predict disposition, dependability, willingness and intelliegence has been a subject of speculation. However, the tendency to classify features of the head, eyes and ears is still prevalent. The tactful, observant handler recognizes that nervous, high-strung horses and sullen, sulky ones require different handling. Colts respond differently than crabby old horses and old, spoiled ones differently than younger, mischievous ones. Indicators that most everyone can learn to detect with practice are found in the horse's age and sex and in the action of ears, eyes, tail and voice.

METHODS

Disposition and behavior will usually indicate the method and severity of the restraint. It is usually advisable to use progressive methods. Start with a passive approach, watch the response and adjust as needed. Often the horse can be convinced by persuasion and passive methods. If not, more progressive methods or a combination of methods may be needed to achieve the desired behavior.

Several methods to try first

Act Tough: A pretense of force is used here in an attempt to out-bluff the horse. A gruff, loud voice is used to get its attention. Grasping a handful of loose skin on the shoulder or jerking the lead rope are methods that may work. Try not to lose your temper and frighten your animal.

Passive Approach: Many old secret concoctions have been used over the years, but to rub armpit perspiration on the horse's nose is still common in taming a horse. Other ideas that might work include:

1. Having a person calm the horse who knows him well.
2. Having a buddy horse near by.
3. Giving him some feed.
4. Talking calmly can also help.

Try it. Anyone of these ideas may get his attention enough so that you can load your pack.

Distactions: To divert his attention from what is being done is another method worth trying. Grasping the ear, with caution, can be quite effective. However, use care in twisting the ear. Nose twitches are used routinely and can be effective, however, watch out and don't get struck. The blindfold is still very effective; use your jacket or whatever is handy but soft on his face and ears. Have everything tied on well when you take the blindfold off!

MILD RESTRAINTS

Hobbles are a useful and practical restraint. Nearly all horses will fight them because they inhibit a natural instinct for flight. Front to front or back to back can be used safely. Tying up a front foot can be used. Here again most horses will fight it and tend to panic. Use large, soft cotton rope to avoid rope burns. The side-line or scotch hobble is used to raise a hind leg. Getting his back foot off the ground helps in loading wild game on a spook!

COMPLETE OR SEVERE RESTRAINTS

These are used as last resorts to get your horse's cooperation. Throwing the horse is only used to shoe a totally uncooperative animal. At best this method is a traumatic experience for the horse, because his escape is completely restricted. Hobbling and side-lining are common methods used to throw an animal.

A war bridle is another type of severe restraint and is only recommended when all else does not work. The war bridle uses applied pressure to the nose, face, mouth and jaw. Progressive pressure may be applied until the desired response is received. Never tie up a horse with a war bridle in place.

Tying up a back foot

For young animals or those hard to pack, tie up a back foot and make life easier for you and your pack animal. Then proceed and load up. A soft cotton rope works well.

See the knots section for doing a bowline around the animal's neck and then a slip knot to tie up the foot.

CHAPTER 8

Basic Wilderness Survival

IMPORTANCE

How important is survival preparedness? It is estimated that one out of three people will face a survival situation some time in his or her life. *You* could be the one out of those three.

Survival is a matter of **life over death.** It is the ability to keep yourself alive when conditions are such that, unless you know what to do, your life may be in danger.

High country weather, extremes in environment and being lost or stranded are very serious situations. Rough terrain and accidental injury can also present serious threats to survival on pack trips.

In a critical outdoor survival situation, how would you respond? Would you be a competent, confident survivor, or would you shrink from the responsibility to yourself and others? Awareness of survival basics can help prepare you to survive both psychologically and intellectually.

GENERAL CONSIDERATIONS

Outdoor activities demand that you be prepared for the unexpected. Challenges to your survival can vary widely. You cannot predict the situations that you may face. However, a number of considerations will help you in dealing with the unexpected.

Your best survival tool is yourself. Prepare yourself both mentally and physically for challenging situations. Preparation, common sense and a determination to survive are your best defenses.

Basic Rules for Survival

1. Tell someone where you are going and when you plan to return.

2. Never go on an outing by yourself.

3. Carry food and water for emergency use.

4. Take a compass and map of the area, and know how to use them. Orient yourself to the map before leaving.

5. Wear proper clothing and equipment. Remember that the weather can change rapidly.

6. Carry other basic survival equipment mentioned below.

7. Plan your outing so that you can return before dark.

Basic Survival Equipment

1. Matches in a waterproof container. It is advisable also to have a backup method for starting a fire, such as flint, tinder and steel wool with 2 AA batteries. A cigarette lighter full of fluid works well.

2. Sharp knife.

3. Compass and map.

4. Reserve quick-energy food source such as candy, nuts or dried fruit.

5. Water, particularly in dry country.

6. Whistle for signaling. Use the coach type. If whistle has metal mouthpiece wrap it with tape so it does not freeze to your lips in cold weather.

7. A lightweight space rescue blanket can be useful for a number of protective purposes.

8. Rain poncho or equivalent.

9. Lightweight flashlight (have spare bulb and batteries).

10. Minimal first aid supplies (Band-Aids, compress bandages, tape, disinfectant and moleskin to name a few).

Primary Needs in a Survival Situation

1. Fire (for warmth and reassurance).

2. Shelter (to preserve body heat and to keep dry).

3. Water (about 2 quarts a day, both summer and winter).

4. Food (starvation is usually not the issue, as humans can go three to six weeks without food, but quick-energy food can become critical in preventing hypothermia).

5. Method for signaling. (Remember: Groups of three whistles or gunshots or signal mirror flashes repeated at regular intevals are signals of distress.)

6. Prevent injury to yourself or your abilities to administer first aid treatment may be in jeopardy.

Be certain that the basic equipment you assemble is adequate to meet these needs. The basic items should be on your person in secure pockets. A **fanny pack or light day pack** can provide space for additional items that might add to your comfort and security. These items might include additional food, a slow-burning candle, an extra knife, nylon rope, a packet of salt, a wire saw, fishing tackle, tissue paper and a pad and pencil. They will do you no good if they are back in the camp, in your vehicle or hanging on your saddle horn if you become separated from your horse.

Clothing

Clothing will vary depending on personal preferences and on the weather, but remember that the weather can change. Wear layers of clothing to adjust to the weather. Wool and some of the outdoor-recommended synthetics are preferable. Appropriate footwear is critical. Sturdy waterproof boots that fit properly and have been broken in are advised. Two pair of socks help to minimize blisters and a pair of extra socks should be carried in case of wet feet. Appropriate headgear is also essential. In cold weather considerable body heat radiates from the head. Winter headgear should conserve heat, breathe and be water-repellent. Summer headgear should provide shade and protection for eyes and ears and ventilation for cooling. Gloves or mittens are a must. Both will help prevent injuries to hands. Mittens will provide more warmth in cold weather than gloves. Waterproofing them is a good practice.

LOST OR STRANDED

Remain calm. Remember that you have prepared yourself for this. Sit down and evaluate your situation. Can you retrace your route? Can you see obvious landmarks consistent with your map? If you are uncertain, admit that you are lost and prepare to spend the night before it is dark. **If lost, the best thing is to stay put.** Moving or wandering around only burns up energy, increases anxiety and makes matters worse. Searchers are much more likely to find you if you stay in one place.

Spend your energy wisely. Pick a sheltered campsite, gather a good supply of firewood and build a small fire. Plan and construct a shelter. A small lean-to shelter can be built from downed branches. Support a ridge pole between two upright poles or in crotches of adjacent trees. More poles can be placed against this pole and covered with branches. Additional protection can be provided from your poncho or space blanket. Place your shelter so that heat will radiate in from your fire. In the winter, snowcaves can be dug. A cave about 3' x 7' will accomodate one person. Care must be taken not to get wet while preparing the cave. Adequate ventilation is needed and can be provided by putting a small hole in the roof of the cave. Locate water and assess your emergency food supply. Check yourself for injuries and blisters and apply appropriate first aid. Improve your shelter if possible. **Rest. Try to stay warm and dry, and stay put.** When appropriate, **use your distress signal** to help searchers locate you.

HYPOTHERMIA AND FROSTBITE

Hypothermia (*hypo,* low: *thermia,* temperature) results from excessive loss of body heat. It is called "the killer of the unprepared" and represents lowering of the inner core temperature of the body. The first sign of hypothermia is uncontrolled shivering followed by vague or slurred speech, fumbling hands or stumbling gait. Due to decreased blood flow to the brain, the next step is irrational judgement and memory loss. Individuals have been known to lose track of where they are, to discard items and even to start removing clothing. At this point a fairly rapid descent into unconsciousness and death can occur.

Four factors are usually present when hypothermia occurs. The first is **cold temperature**, although severe cold is not required. Temperatures well above freezing can initiate critical body heat loss when combined with other factors. **Wetness** resulting from rain or snow, immersion or perspiration accelerates heat loss. Also, **wind and the resulting chill factors** can greatly decrease the apparent temperature. A likely victim for hypothermia is an individual who is **exhausted** and who has unwisely wasted body energy reserves.

Field treament includes moving the victim to a sheltered area, removing wet clothing and replacing with dry clothing or placing victim in a sleeping bag. These measures are intended to stop heat loss. Heat can be restored to the victim by having someone get into the sleeping bag with him or her to begin warming by direct skin-to-skin contact. If the victim is conscious, warm fluid and quick-energy food should be given. Do not administer alcohol! As the victim recovers, keep him warm and dry and proceed to medical help as soon as possible. In severe cases with greatly lowered body temperatures, cardiac arrest may occur on warming. An individual trained in cardiopulmonary resuscitation (CPR) should monitor the victim and provide treatment if necessary.

Know your enemy. Never underestimate the power of cold, dampness and wind. Do not overestimate your own strength or that of your party. One individual mishap can pin you to a location where you are exposed to harsh elements.

Frostbite may occur with hypothermia or independently. To prevent frostbite keep your hands, feet and exposed areas warm, dry and protected from the wind. Check frequently for numbness or a change in skin color to gray or to yellow-white spots. Do not rub frostbite areas with snow, as it will only cause injury. Warm affected areas by placing next to your abdominal region or other areas of your body. If you get wet, dry yourself and your clothes immediately.

DEHYDRATION

Dehydration occurs as water evaporates from your body without adequate replacement. The blood thickens, causing strain on the heart; tissue cells may die from lack of water. In a desert or hot area you must take precautions against overexposure to the sun. You may be affected by sunburn, heat exhaustion or heat stroke. All may be prevented by staying out of the sun and avoiding overexertion. Avoid sweating, as this uses body fluid rapidly. Carry water in your stomach, not in your canteen. If you are thirsty, drink. Saving water if you are already becoming dehydrated will do no good. If you are short of water, do not eat food, because water will be used in digestion. If extended exposure to hot weather extremes occur, **sleep during the day and walk during cooler hours.** Daytime cooling can be achieved by digging about 30" into the soil. Lie down inside the hole and cover yourself. Even though air temperatures are high, the ground temperature below the surface should be considerably cooler.

WATER

A frequent source of water is essential to survival. **You need 2 to 4 quarts each day**, although you may survive up to a few days without water. There is a sharp distinction between water for survival and water for convenient outdoor use. **In general you should consider all outdoor water potentially contaminated.** There are a number of disease-causing microbes from both animal and human sources that may be present in untreated water. Even water that looks fresh and clear may carry these microbes. If possible water should be treated before use. **Boiling** for three minutes plus one minute for each 100' of elevation is minimal for safety. Boil for at least 30 minutes. **Chemicals for water treatment, water-purifying filter pumps and filtering straws** can be purchased at sporting goods stores. Finding water in arid conditions can be difficult. Look for plants that thrive on water and for animals that live near water. Dig in shady portions of dry stream beds. Look for springs at the base of cliffs or for potholes in bedrock. Dew can be sponged from plants early in the morning. In critical survival situations, replenishing fluid in your body is more important than assuring that the water is free of disease-causing organisms.

STARVATION

Humans can survive for many days and even a few weeks without food. Food requirements are not as critical as are those for water. However, you will be more efficient, alert and confident if you can satisfy your hunger. There are sources of food in nearly any area you may pack into. It may be necessary to change your way of thinking to recognize them. Generally, anything that birds and animals eat will be safe and have some value. Your gun or fishing equipment provides the best means of a meal. Additionally, you can learn how to make and use snares, traps, deadfalls, nets, slingshots and spears. You can also become familiar with plant foods in your area. However, identification of edible plants can be difficult, and unless you learn to identify them in advance, it may be better to avoid plants as food. Books providing information on edible plants are available from your local library or bookstore. It is much better to have emergency food with you as part of your survival equipment. **Always carry food items in your fanny pack.**

PREPAREDNESS TRAINING

These few pages offer only mininal survival information. It must be stressed that the **DETERMINATION TO SURVIVE is the most important factor in survival.** Some information is better than no information at all. It is strongly recommended that individuals involved in outdoor activities take advantage of survival training opportunities in their community. Such training may be available from the state game and fish department, organizations such as the National Ski Patrol or from various outdoor clubs. All outdoorsmen should also have advanced first aid training available from the American Red Cross. Training in CPR is also highly recommended.

Many of the ideas expressed in this section have been freely taken from survival manuals prepared by the Colorado Department of Natural Resources Division of Wildlife and by the Wyoming Game and Fish Department.

CHAPTER 9

Regulations and Agency Information

Professional Outfitting and Guiding on Public Lands

If you are interested in becoming a licensed outfitter, a number of things must be considered. Every state has its own regulations, applications and procedures. In the state of Wyoming, all the agencies involved with public lands have coordinated their efforts and prepared a Memorandum of Understanding between the following agencies:

The U.S. Department of the Interior
Bureau of Land Management - Wyoming State Office
And
The U.S. Department of Agriculture
USDA Forest Service - Rocky Mountain Region
USDA Forest Service - Intermountain Region
And
The Wyoming State Board of Outfitters and Professional Guides
And
Office of State Lands and Investments
And
The Wyoming Game and Fish Commission
And
U.S. Department of the Interior - Fish and Wildlife Service
And
U.S. Department of the Interior - National Park Service
Grand Teton National Park
Concerning

Maintaining and enhancing the quality of service provided by the outfitter industry in Wyoming through the coordinated application of state and federal laws and regulations governing the operating of outfitting and guiding services.

Depending upon what agency you need to deal with, one must figure a minimum of 30 days and most likely a waiting period of 90 plus days before your permit is approved and authorization is given. Applications and other paperwork might include such things as:

- Special Use Permit
- Annual Evaluation of that Permit
- Post Use Report
- Operating Plan for Commercial Outfitters and Competitive Permittees
- Outfitters-Guides Performance Rating

Other forms may be required, depending on the agency that has jurisdiction over the public lands where you plan to visit.

Whether you plan to outfit or guide on public lands or private lands in Wyoming, you must go through the Wyoming State Board of Outfitters and Professional Guides office in Cheyenne, Wyoming, for the proper applications and regulations. **Contact: 1-800-264-0981 or outfitters.state.wy.us**

Some permits are for specified sites, and certain fees are to be assessed depending on the number of days and number of guests using the area.

Whether you are applying to be a professional outfitter or guide or you are just planning a trip for family and friends, you need to find out the rules and regulations that pertain to the area you plan to pack into. Wilderness areas are different than state or other federal lands.

There are numerous state and federal laws and regulations governing the operation of outfitting and guiding services, and many different agencies have the authority to enforce them. Some fees are based on the number of heartbeats in your party, (includes man, horse, dogs, etc.).

Before you go into an area you are not familiar with, call, write, e-mail and get informed, so you are fully prepared. See the appendixes for samples of the types of information required by some, not all, of the authorizing agencies involved. Note also that there are fees attached to most applications. This information is a part of the memorandum of understanding described above.

PACKING IN BEAR COUNTRY

If you have ever hunted in bear country and entered a thick patch of dark timber and ran onto a fresh track of a grizzly, you will know that the hair on the back of your neck stands straight out! I found myself trying to look in all directions at the same time and trying to exit that timber quickly! Grizzlies are awesome, powerful and temperamental creatures. We must give them our utmost respect and do everything possible to avoid a confrontation. Because of the increasing numbers of bears and more encounters, this information was put together to help outdoorsmen better prepare to avoid potentially dangerous situations.

Food Storage and Sanitation Orders are available from the USDA Forest Service, and you should obtain a copy if you plan to take a trip into any country where bears exist. Below are a few of their regulations. The basis of these orders is to prevent bears from being attracted to camp sites, campgrounds, trailheads, picnic sites and other areas where people congregate.

What must be stored properly?

Any human food (including canned food, soft drinks and alcoholic beverages); harvested game animals and parts; pet food, processed livestock feed and grains; and personal hygiene items such as soap, toothpaste and deodorants. This also includes garbage and empty food and beverage containers.

How do you store the above items?

You must place food and other items in bear resistant containers or hard-sided vehicles or suspend the food and container at least 10' above the ground and 4' from any vertical support.

What are considered bear resistant containers?

The heavy metal boxes in some campgrounds and bear resistant horse panniers are acceptable for storing food items. These containers must be certified by the Interagency Grizzly Bear Committee Courtesy Inspection Program. Leather or canvas panniers are not considered to be bear proof.

How do you store game meat and parts?

Harvested big game animals and parts thereof must be at least 100 yards from a sleeping area, recreation site or National Forest System Trail. If you store game meat on the ground and unattended, it must be at least one-half mile away from sleeping or recreation sites and at least 200 yards from a national forest system trail. Small game and fish should be stored in the same manner.

What are meat and food poles, and how do I use them?

Meat and food poles are placed at some trailheads and back country sites for the safety of visitors. Whether provided or you make up your own, they must be at least 10' high, and you must place your food or game items at least 4' away from the upright tree. Separate ropes are usually used for each item that is pulled up to the pole and then tied tight to the tree so a bear cannot undue the rope and lower the food container or meat from the pole.

Request additional information if your pack trip is going into bear country. Contact the USDA Forest Service or other agency with the authority for the area you plan to visit. The above are some of the very basics and in no way should be considered to include all the information that is needed and required in bear country. If you plan ahead and heed all the regulations you should not be bothered by bears. If you do not adhere to the regulations you could be sited and receive a fine of up to $10,000.

SAMPLE OUTFITTER'S LETTER TO A POTENTIAL CLIENT

Savage Run Outfitters
Jay Talbott
2122 Reynolds
Laramie, WY 82070
(307) 742-9004

Dear Sir:

Thank you for your inquiry!

We are a small, family-operated outfitting business, specializing in three-day mountain lion and antelope hunts. Most hunters choose to stay in a motel in Laramie. We furnish four-wheel-drive vehicles, spotting scopes, the noon meal and dogs for the lion hunts.

Since season dates vary from year to year and area to area, let us know your plans, and we will work with you.

We will gladly furnish references and assist you in filling out hunting applications.

Wyoming licenses are on a computer drawing basis, so you need to have your applications to the Wyoming Game and Fish Department in early January. I am sending a brochure with more details concerning licensing deadlines, dates, pictures and our price list.

We make only one guarantee, that you will enjoy your hunt.

Sincerely,

Savage Run Outfitters,
Jay Talbott

State Outfitters License No. 88

TREE-SAVER STRAPS AND HITCH LINE

Here is another way to tie up your animals.

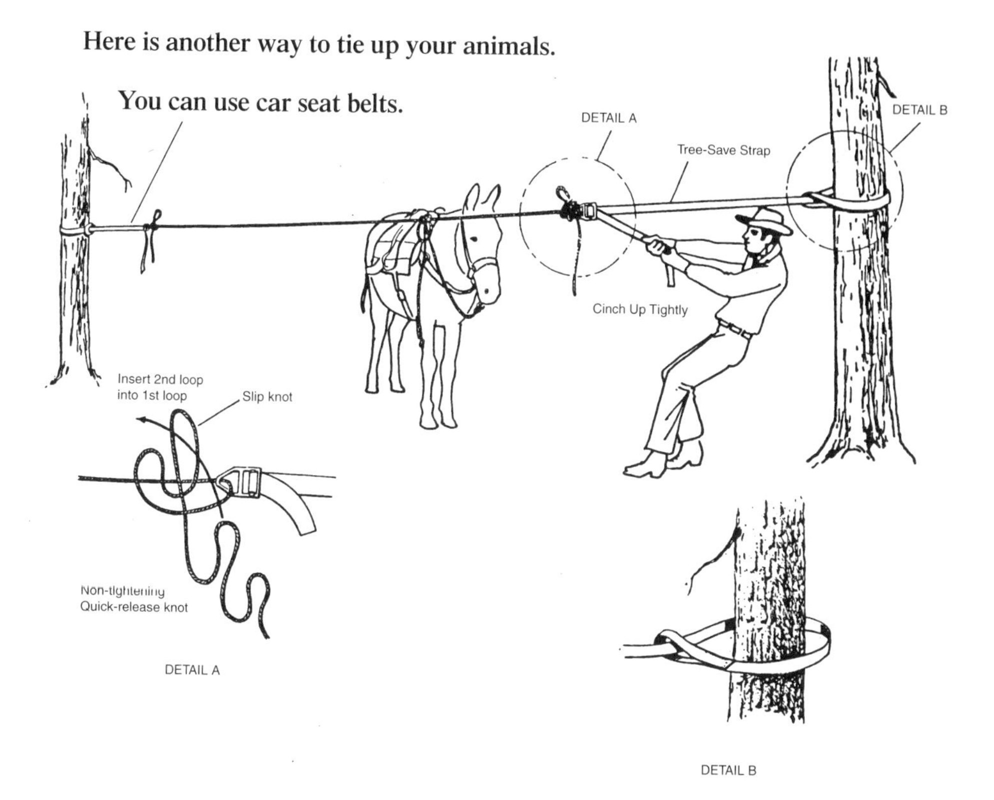

How to Use:

1. Choose a durable spot. Hard and rocky ground is the best.
2. Place the tree-savers and rope about 6’ to 7’ above the ground.
3. Stretch the line tightly between two trees, using adjustable nylon tree-saver straps.
4. Run the rope between the straps; tie with a quick-release knot and pull tight.
5. Tie stock to the high line about 7’ apart and at least 6’ from the trees.

Why Use Them?

1. Keeps ropes from damaging bark on trees.
2. Saves tree roots from being damaged by closely tied horses who may paw the ground, uncovering roots.
3. Gives horses more area to move around.
4. Less damage to native plants is done when horses are tied on rocky ground.

TYING TO THE HITCH LINE

If horses are only tied with a slip knot to the high line rope, they can move freely, and the lead rope will slip and move with them and horses can crowd up. Knots can be put in the high line rope, or a variety of products such as the knot eliminator shown here can be attached to the rope to prevent the lead rope from slipping back and forth.

OUR PUBLIC LANDS

Many of our public lands have been created for multiple use for all to use and enjoy. There are many demands, many users and many philosophies as to the best management of these lands. Here are a few thoughts on sharing and caring for these valuable resources.

1. Share the trails, trail heads and popular camp sites with a positive, friendly attitude. Be a good neighbor!

2. Do not make new trails by cutting across switchbacks and through soft meadows.

3. Clean up campsites thoroughly and replace fire rings. Leave no trace!

4. Adhere to the 200' guideline. Keep your camp and stock 200' from water and other camps and your toilet 200' from camp, water and the trail.

5. Be courteous on the trail and yield when possible.

6. Abide by the rules and regulations for the area you are visiting.

7. Scatter manure before you leave your campsite so others are not offended.

There is enough room for all the many uses and users if we all do our part to conserve, clean up and protect. Totally locking up these lands on one hand or abusing them on the other is not good and makes no sense. So we must all pledge to use, share and to care for these precious resources owned by all of us.

Certified Noxious Weed-Free Hay and Straw Requirements

Anyone using our national forests and/or national grasslands needs to comply by only packing in hay or straw that has been certified as noxious weed and seed free by a certified state or county agricultural officer at the weed and pest office. Processed hay cubes and/or grain are okay as the weed seeds are killed during the processing. States have different methods of identifying the certified bales. Two examples are different color twine or sticky orange tags. The use of certified hay or straw is required on some state and federal lands and is recommended on others. Contact the agency involved to confirm this regulation. **It is a good practice for all packers to use certified hay or straw, whether required or recommended. Help keep our forests free of noxious weeds by doing your part!**

Canadian Thistle

Dalmation Toadflax

Leafy Spurge

Whitetop

Russian Knapweed

These are a few of the more undesireable noxious weeds.

Putting it to use: Packing lumber is a challenge.

REFERENCES

1. Back, Joe, *Horses, Hitches and Rocky Trails*, Chicago, Illinois, The Swallow Press, Inc., 1959.

2. Davis, Francis W., *Horse Packing in Pictures*, Charles Scribner's Sons, New York, 1975.

3. Durrell, L.W., *Packing and Outfitting*, Colorado State University.

4. Hatley, George B., and Joe B. Johnson, *How to Pack a Horse*, Pullman, Washington: Washington State University, EM2627, June 1966.

5. Hill, Oliver C., *A Deluxe Pack Trip*, 1970.

6. Hill, Oliver C., *Packing and Outfitting Field Manual,* Fourth Edition, 1989.

7. Nicholls, J.M., Wyoming State 4-H Leader, *4-H Ropecraft*, 4-H Bulletin No. 41001, 1973.

8. Richardson, Allen G., Riding and Packing Instructor, Animal Science Department, Colorado State University, 1970.

9. Sansom, Bonnie Dale, *Sourdough Good Eating*, University of Nevada, Bulletin C-35, October 1964.

10. Reynolds, Douglas A., *Persuasion, Restraint, Subjection*, University of Nevada Publication, June 1975.

11. Colorado Department of Natural Resources, Division of Wildlife, Survival Manual.

12. Wyoming Game and Fish Department, Survival Manual.

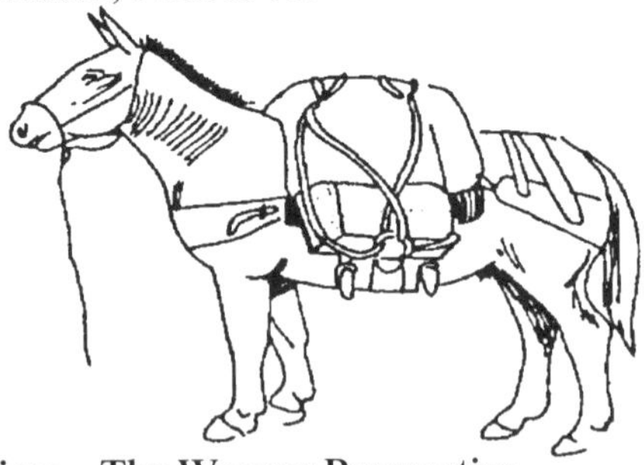

13. Wyoming Travel and Tourism – The Wagner Perspective, Cheyenne, Wyoming.

14. Wyoming State Board of Outfitters and Professional Guides, Cheyenne, Wyoming.

15. USDA Forest Service.

16. Albany County Weed and Pest Control District, Laramie, Wyoming, and Montana State University for weed photos.

APPENDIXES

Sample Agency Forms

1. Application for Temporary Use Permit
   State of Wyoming Board of Land Commissioners
2. Outfitter Permit Verification and Area Authorization
   USDA Forest Service
3. Special Recreation Application and Permit
   U.S. Department of the Interior, BLM
4. Special Recreation Permit Post Use Report
   U.S. Department of the Interior, BLM
5. Letter on the Process to Obtain an Outfitter's License
   Wyoming State Board of Outfitters and
   Professional Guides

NOTE: These forms are examples only. Most agencies change their forms regularly. Contact each agency for the most current forms, regulations and procedures.

PERMIT APPLICATION FEE $25.00

STATE OF WYOMING

BOARD OF LAND COMMISSIONERS

APPLICATION FOR TEMPORARY USE PERMIT

APPLICATION NO. ____________________ COUNTY ____________

Assigned by office

APPLICANT:

Name ____________________

Address ____________________

____

Phone ____________________

Use applied for: (check one)

[ ] Construction activity (indicate total acreage affected ____________

[ ] Hot mix facility

[ ] Organized recreation activity

[ ] Roadway (indicate proposed width ________ and length ________)

[ ] Sign Board

[ ] Stockpile site

[ ] Water removal facility

[ ] Outfitting/guiding activities (indicate exclusive _____ or nonexclusive _____ and provide outfitting/guiding license no. ____________)

[ ] Other: (specify) ____________________

Specifically describe proposed use: ____________________

____

List any improvements to be placed on the land: ____________________

____

Describe the state land applied for and delineate the proposed permit area on the attached plat: (use separate sheet if necessary for the description)

____

____

Will the proposed use result in loss of production, unusable or inaccessible land or water, surface disturbance or damage to crops or improvements:

Yes ______ No ______ If yes, describe: ____________________

____

____

Requested duration of permit: From ____________ To ____________

Date Date

Consideration offered for permit: ____________________

I hereby certify that I have read and agree to abide by the rules and regulations of the Board of Land Commissioners governing temporary use permits and the terms and conditions of the temporary use permit if one is issued to me.

____________________ ____________

Signature of Applicant Date

____

Print or Type Name

MOST FORESTS EXCEPT THE BRIDGER-TETON

United States Department of Agriculture	Forest Service	______ District ______ National Forest	______________ P.O. Box ________ ________, WY _____

Reply to: 2720 Date: ____________

Subject: Outfitter Permit Verification and Area Authorization

To: Wyoming State Board of Outfitters and Professional Guides
1750 Westland Road
Cheyenne, WY 82002

I certify that a temporary special use permit/use for sheep moose goat lion spring bear (circle appropriate one(s)) spike camp will be issued to ______________________ for outfitting and guiding on the ________ National Forest for the 19__ season; provided that the permittee submits an annual itinerary, copy of insurance, pays the required fees, and obtains the proper State outfitter license and hunt area authorization from the Board.

I request that ____________________ be granted a hunt area authorization for the following in conjunction with the aforementioned permit/use.

Species	Hunt Unit
______________________	______________________
______________________	______________________

This hunt area authorization is temporary for one season only.

If the Board has any recommendations relating to this issuance, please contact ____________________ at the ________________ District Office with your recommendations.

______________________________________ ____________________________

DISTRICT RANGER DATE

Form 8370-1
(May 1996)

UNITED STATES
DEPARTMENT OF THE INTERIOR
BUREAU OF LAND MANAGEMENT

FORM APPROVED
OMB NO. 1004-0119
Expires: September 30, 1998

SPECIAL RECREATION APPLICATION AND PERMIT
(43 U.S.C 1201; 43 U.S.C. 1701; 16 U.S.C. 460 L-6(a); and 43 CFR Group 8300)

Permit No.

Instructions: Complete Items 1 through 8, and return to appropriate BLM Office. *(Use additional sheets, if necessary.)*

Type or Print Plainly in Ink

WHEN SIGNED BY AUTHORIZED BLM OFFICIAL, THIS PERMIT AUTHORIZES

1. Name of person and/or organization

Address *(include zip code)*

Telephone No. *(include area code)* Business Residence

2. To use the following public lands *(provide name, legal description and/or attach map).*

3. For the following purpose *(provide full description of activity or event including number of anticipated participants and spectators).*

4. During the following times and dates *(specify below)*

ARRIVAL			DEPARTURE		
DATE *(Mon., Day, Yr.)*	TIME		DATE *(Mon., Day, Yr.)*	DEPARTURE	
	AM	PM		AM	PM

5. Type of permit: ❑ Commercial ❑ Non-commercial ❑ Other OHV events with 50 or more vehicles ❑ Other *(list type)* ________
❑ Competitive ❑ Non-competitive ❑ Individual/Private

6. Facilities *(describe facilities including water and sanitation facilities you intend to provide, attach plans and location maps).*

7a. Previous permits: Have you been issued a permit for a previous event or activity (If "yes," answer the following.)

b. BLM Office issuing permit

c. Date of latest permit

d. Have you, or your organization, forfeited any portion of any previous permit, bond, or surety submitted for use of public lands, or is any investigation or legal action pending against you or your organization for use of public lands? ❑ Yes ❑ No *(if "yes," attach details on separate sheet.)*

8. Certification of Information: I CERTIFY That the information given by me in this application is true, complete, and correct to the best of my knowledge and belief and is given in good faith. I acknowledge that I (we) am (are) required to comply with any conditions or stipulations that are required by the authorized officer when the permit is issued.

(Signature of Applicant) (Date)

Title 18 U.S.C. Section 1001, makes it a crime for any person knowingly and willfully to make to any department or agency of the United States any false, fictitious, or fraudulent statements or representations as to any matter within its jurisdiction.

This application is hereby approved subject to the conditions and special stipulations on reverse and any attachments.

(Signature of Authorized Official) (Date)

PERMITTEE MUST HAVE THIS PERMIT *(OR LEGIBLE COPY) IN POSSESSION DURING USE IN PERMITTED AREAS.*

United States Department of the Interior
Bureau of Land Management
Wyoming State Office

Special Recreation Permit Post Use Report

Name:________________________ **Year:**____________
SRP Number:____________________ **Expires:**____________

Use Fee Calculations (Instructions on reverse)

1. Total Gross Income[a] .... $ ____________

2. Deductions[b]
   a. Transportation .... $ ____________
   b. Lodging .... $ ____________

3. Total of lines 2a and 2b .... $ ____________

4. Line 1 Minus Line 3 .... $ ____________

5. Non Public Lands Use Adjustment[c]
   a. Percent of Total-Use that Occurred on BLM Land ... ____________
   b. Fee Adjustment Factor[c] ... ____________

6. Adjusted Gross Income (Line 4 times Line 5b) .... $ ____________

7. Use Fees[d] (Line 6 times .03) .... $ ____________

8. Credit from Previous Year/Advance Payment[e] .... $ ____________

9. Amount Due[e] BLM/Credit .... $ ____________

SAMPLE

Visitor Use Data:

Number of Days on BLM ____________

Number of Participants ____________

____________________ ____________
Permittee's Signature Date

I certify that the information provided by me in this Post Use Report is true, accurate, and complete to the best of my knowledge.

____________________ ____________
Authorized Officer Date

Hunt Area Used/No. Hunters (i.e., 42/8, 74/6 etc.)

Antelope ____________

Deer ____________

Bear ____________

Elk ____________

Moose ____________

Sheep ____________

Lion ____________

Other Uses ____________

APPENDIX 5

DAVE D. FREUDENTHAL
GOVERNOR

Wyoming State Board of Outfitters and Professional Guides

JANE E. FLAGG
ADMINISTRATOR

November 17, 2004

Dear:

I am writing in regards to your request on the process of obtaining an outfitter's license. New applicants must take a closed book exam as is required by W.S. 23-2-413(b). You must submit the enclosed application, operation plan and proof of lawful presence (see attached notice) with the $500 new applicant fee. This fee is non-refundable. The study material is then sent to you. If you fail the exam you may re-take it again in thirty days.

You may call or write the Board to schedule a time to take the exam. The test is given from either 8:00 a.m. – 12:00 p.m. or 1:00 p.m. – 5:00 p.m. at the Board office in Cheyenne. You must test for June 30th of the current year to obtain a license for that year. Your test results will be available the day after you take the exam (or on the next Monday if taken on a Friday).

Upon passing the exam you must submit the following information at least two weeks prior to the Board meeting you plan to attend:

1. A letter stating your guiding experience if you have not guided in the State of Wyoming. The Board requires a minimum of one year's experience, however they may accept similar experience.

2. Letters of intent from the BLM and/or Forest Service indicating they will issue you permits for the areas and species requested on your Operation Plan.

3. If you plan on operating on private land you must submit the proper forms and maps as required per the Board's rules and regulations which must also match the species and areas on your Operation Plan.

4. A letter from your insurance company indicating they will insure you in accordance with W.S. 23-2-411(d). If your license is approved you will need to submit a certificate of insurance showing the Board as a certificate holder.

5. License fee ($500) if approved.

6. If you are purchasing a business from another outfitter, that outfitter must submit a letter relinquishing his license (or areas of operation if he holds other permits).

7. If you intend to operate on any land that intermingles with state land you will need to contact the State Land Office for an application and submit a copy of the application with your other paperwork.

All outfitters are required to state their refund policy on their initial application. Although the Board does not dictate how you should write your policy, you might want to be aware that a large portion of complaints filed against outfitters are refund disputes. If you require a deposit you may want to list those circumstances under which refunds are returned. Please be apprised that the Game & Fish Commission recently changed their regulations to allow medical problems (with documentation) as a basis for the refund of hunting license fees. This could have a bearing on how you address refunds. Some terms you may want consider when writing your refund policy are enclosed.

All new applicants must appear before the Board for approval. A camp and equipment inspection will be made if requested by the Board or their investigators. If you should have any questions or need any help, please do not hesitate to contact me.

Sincerely,

Jane Flagg, Administrator

Enc. Application
Operation Plan
Citizenship Notice
Refund Policy Information

1950 BLUEGRASS CIRCLE, STE 280 CHEYENNE, WY 82002 FAX: 307-777-6715 PHONE: 307-635-1589
Or: 1-800-264-0981

NOTES

NOTES